AWAKENING

A Journey Within

Georges and Judith Arseneau

BALBOA.PRESS
A DIVISION OF HAY HOUSE

Copyright © 2020 Georges and Judith Arseneau.

All rights reserved. No part of this book may be used or reproduced by any means, graphic, electronic, or mechanical, including photocopying, recording, taping or by any information storage retrieval system without the written permission of the author except in the case of brief quotations embodied in critical articles and reviews.

Balboa Press books may be ordered through booksellers or by contacting:

Balboa Press
A Division of Hay House
1663 Liberty Drive
Bloomington, IN 47403
www.balboapress.com
844-682-1282

Because of the dynamic nature of the Internet, any web addresses or links contained in this book may have changed since publication and may no longer be valid. The views expressed in this work are solely those of the author and do not necessarily reflect the views of the publisher, and the publisher hereby disclaims any responsibility for them.

The author of this book does not dispense medical advice or prescribe the use of any technique as a form of treatment for physical, emotional, or medical problems without the advice of a physician, either directly or indirectly. The intent of the author is only to offer information of a general nature to help you in your quest for emotional and spiritual well-being. In the event you use any of the information in this book for yourself, which is your constitutional right, the author and the publisher assume no responsibility for your actions.

Cover art and illustrations by Jeanette Haynes

Scripture quotations marked (KJV) are taken from the
KING JAMES VERSION, public domain.

Unless otherwise noted, all scriptures and/ or paraphrases are from the JERUSALEM BIBLE Copyright© 1966, 1967, 1968 by Darton, Longmand & Todd LTD and Doubleday and Co. Inc. All rights reserved.

Print information available on the last page.

ISBN: 978-1-9822-5820-7 (sc)
ISBN: 978-1-9822-5819-1 (hc)
ISBN: 978-1-9822-5818-4 (e)

Library of Congress Control Number: 2020922625

Balboa Press rev. date: 12/21/2020

This book is dedicated to all the courageous Souls coming to this beautiful planet to be of service to humanity at this very important time in our evolution. May you continue to respond to that eternal call of your heart to be a part of the answer. May the Light of The Infinite One guide your steps forever.

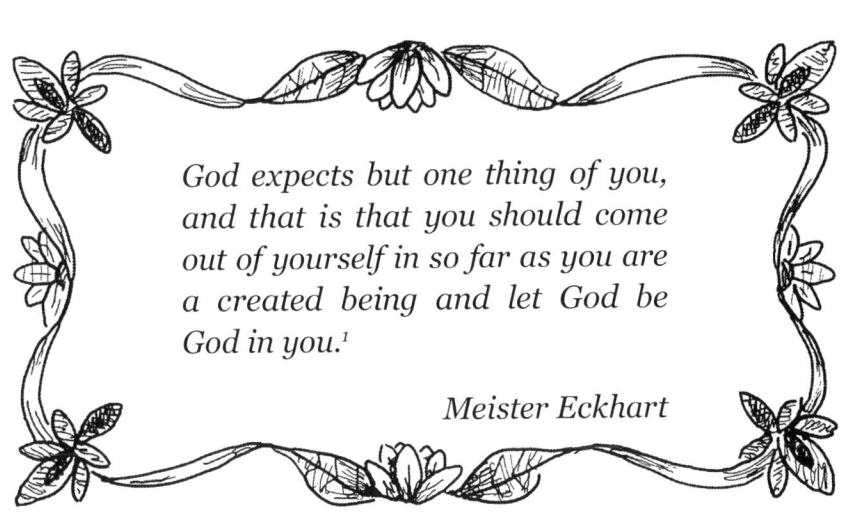

God expects but one thing of you, and that is that you should come out of yourself in so far as you are a created being and let God be God in you.[1]

Meister Eckhart

Contents

Introduction	xi
A Child of God	1
The Divine Artist	5
Through the Eyes of a Prince	9
Lift Up Thine Eyes	13
We Are One	17
From the Beginning	21
The Promise of the Sun	25
The Divine Invitation	29
Passion for the Divine	35
Inside There is a Light	39
The Smile of the Sun	45
For One Soul	49
The Promised Land	53
Prayer of St Francis	57
Home is Where the Heart is	59
Homeward Bound	63
In the Beginning	67
I Am With You Always	73
The Silent Visitor	79
A Dream of Oneness	85
Answering the Call Within	89
Awakening	93
The Light of the Sun	99
The Year of Awakening	103
The Blessing of Fullness	107
The Little Chalice	111

Love is Forever	115
The Manger of the Heart	119
Time for Change	123
Ablaze With Love	127
Prayer of Teresa of Avila	131
The Treasure of the Heart	133
This is the Day	137
I Am With You	141
The Light of Love	145
The Secret of Shalimar	151
Love Ye One Another	155
Steps of Joy	159
The Tinker's Gift	163
Lead Me to the Real	167
Paradise Found	171
Truth is the Way	175
Once There Was a Man	179
The Minstrel	183
The Year of Acceptance	185
Proclamation of Peace	189
Peace on Earth	191
Loving God is All There Is	195
The Promise	199
The Doe	203
Time to Live	207
Unto the Least of These	211
The Dream Restored	219
Please, Where is Love?	223
The Journey Home	229
Epilogue	235
References	239
Acknowledgements	245
About the Authors	247

Introduction

Throughout the history of this planet, stories or parables that would speak to the Heart were told and passed down from person to person. They were meant to inspire us to set out on our own journey – a journey that would continue, as we would progressively awaken to who we really are.

Our only desire is for you, the reader, to immerse yourselves in these stories, and as you read them, to live them as if they are your own. They are meant to be read by the Heart, not so much by the mind. If there is one story that speaks to you and inspires you to set out on your own journey within and awaken to who you are – a pure innocent Child of God, then the book has fulfilled its purpose.

Thank you for the opportunity to share part of who we are with you. We will always be grateful for this opportunity.

A Child of God

It was the kind of beautiful Spring day that one dreams about, bright, warm, and sunny. Everything was teeming with life, vibrant and alive. As a young man walked the path, he could smell the fragrance of flowers that filled the air and hear the sounds of new life awakening. Looking out over the valley, he could see a beautiful rainbow of colors in the blossoms that covered the land like frosting on a cake. Birds were singing songs of joy, and every living creature was alive and filled with Love. It was as if he could hear Mother Nature herself, laughing and giggling, playing with her newborn child of Spring. As he continued down the path, he began to think back at how long it had been since he had felt this close to nature. Memories of his early childhood began to stir within him. He remembered himself as a very young boy, lying in fields of tall grass, gazing at the clouds, feeling totally One with his surroundings. As these memories surfaced, he started to feel the responsibility and problems of his work enter his mind. The joyous feeling of the Spring day began to fade as he began to dwell once more on the problems and questions that faced him.

These were the very problems that he had tried to forget by coming here to walk this land and to be in the midst of nature. He thought about how as a child growing older, he had lost that joy by feeling that he had to be serious and concentrate on his problems. When his friends wanted to play and roam through the fields, he told them he had better things to do with his time. Now, he remembered clearly: it was at that moment that he felt the child in him, the one who wanted to play and be free, begin to die.

There he stood on the path, wondering what he could do to recapture the feelings of his early youth without having the problems in his life overwhelm him anymore. Just then, he heard the sound of magical laughter coming from a clearing right off the path. He went ahead to the edge of the trees, looked into the clearing, and saw a young child running through a field of bright flowers, laughing and chasing butterflies. It was the most beautiful and alive child he had ever seen, as beautiful as all of nature herself. The child seemed to be One with all of the surroundings, floating from flower to flower like the butterflies, and running through the tall grasses as gracefully as the wind. He wanted to run into the field and be with the child, but a part of him was holding back, afraid of what others would think if they were to see him playing and chasing butterflies. He felt torn between these two parts within himself and started to become very frustrated and angry with himself. He could not stand there watching the child any longer. He turned and ran back down the path, away from the clearing. The frustration and anger became more intense. He could not go any further. He stood motionless, frozen in fear, feeling himself being pulled by both parts; one wanting to express the child within, and the other wanting to run. He closed his eyes and prayed to God to help him let go of the fear and frustration that held him so tightly. Just then the words that The Christ said so long ago came to him, *"Lest ye become as little children, ye cannot enter the kingdom of heaven."*[2] In that instant, he knew that he must go back and find that child who had been playing in the clearing.

The fear left his body in a great rush. He kicked off his shoes, threw off his jacket, and began to run back towards the clearing. As he approached the field, he could see the child sitting under a tree. As soon as he started to walk across the field, the child stood up with open arms and began to run towards him. They met in the middle of the field and embraced in a loving hug. At that very moment, something miraculous happened. The child and he became One. They were no longer separate. He found himself merging, dissolving into that radiant child of God that he had abandoned so long ago, and who had waited patiently for this very moment when they could once again be together.

Everything around him took on a new wonder and beauty as he looked through the eyes of the child within himself. He ran through the meadow, feeling totally connected with every living thing. He felt like God Himself was holding him in His arms like a newborn child. Never before had he felt this alive. He knew that he would never let that child in him die again. He was totally One with everything – full of wonderment and joy. It was true. He was, and always would be, a child of God.

The Divine Artist

Summer is approaching fast. The birds are singing their sweet songs of love. The flowers are blossoming in their richness. The array of colors is spectacular, from the vivid greens and blues to the pastel shades of yellow, pink, and purple. This planet is truly a magnificent masterpiece of art, painted by a most loving Artist …

Once there was a small, little girl who, when viewing a golden-red sunset painted in the sky, decided to go on a journey to find this Artist. She knew the Artist must have been filled with Love, for such a gift inspired so many people and brought tears of joy and happiness to the hearts of all. She began one early morning, dressed in baggy jeans, a summer top, and old worn sandals. First, she came upon a meadow, filled with tiny purple flowers. The fragrance was overwhelming. It was so sweet! She sat by the flowers for a long time and knew these were painted by the very same Artist who made the sunset.

"Can you show me who painted you?" she asked. The flowers swayed as if chanting a beautiful tune of love and gratitude. Then … silence. It was so still. She listened. "Look within and you will find the Artist," she heard. Startled, and a little apprehensive, she got up and slowly walked from the meadow. What did that mean? She went on.

Soon, she found herself on a narrow path which led up to a beautiful mountain. Just as she had turned the corner, she saw standing before her a delicate brown deer. It didn't move. Its eyes were compassionate pools of love. She began to get lost in them. She felt so much love she was about to cry, as she spontaneously touched the warm neck of this beautiful creature. So solid and all-knowing, yet so gentle and clear. Surely, the same Artist had to have also made this example of pure Love. So she asked the deer, "Please tell me, how can I possibly find the Artist that made you? You are so lovely. I feel only love when I gaze upon you." The deer looked straight into her eyes. It got very silent. The little girl jumped back. She was frightened. She was feeling too much. Her heart was pounding; she felt like fainting, she was melting into an infinite abyss of Love. Where was the deer? Where was she?

A voice whispered in her heart, "Look within, look within and you will find the Artist." She remembered she had heard that before. Those words mystified her even more now. She kept thinking, "Look within, what does that really mean?" She looked up into the fluffy clouds and asked to know. "Please," she yelled out loud, "Please, dear Artist, show yourself!" The clouds parted, and a beautiful little goldfinch flew down, sat on her shoulder, and sang a melody which touched the depths of her very soul. She had to meet this Artist and to thank the Creator of such beauty.

The Love she had in her heart was all-consuming. The little goldfinch sensed her question even before she said it. Then the small girl spoke again, "I see you are so beautiful, little goldfinch. You must know who painted you. Please tell me. I have to tell this Artist that such a Love has grown in my heart just by seeing all this beauty. I cannot be silent anymore. I must see the Artist! I must Love!"

The Divine Artist

Suddenly, the goldfinch began to change. The trees, birds, flowers, all seemed to stop and pause. Rays of light came out through the little bird's heart. There was a brilliant glowing Light, growing and swirling until it encompassed the little girl with baggy jeans and worn sandals. She heard an echo of these words, "Dear little one of Light, look within, look within. I Am Here." She closed her eyes. Light and colors, stars, purple flowers, delicate deer, golden-Light goldfinch, and a small girl, were all there. Then, from the very center of all those forms emerged the Sun. Time stood still. Everything fell away and she was in the very Sun. She was floating in Love Itself. She could only say, "Thank you, I love you, dear Artist, I love You." And for one moment, she knew all life as if it were her very own. She knew the trees, the butterflies, the flowers, the birds. She knew happiness and Love. She knew herself. She knew the Artist. She smiled a smile that would endure forever. She knew Love.

Through the Eyes of a Prince

It was a warm and beautiful day. The air was filled with the fragrance of delicate flowers and the freshness of the gentle breeze. All was perfect in this Kingdom of Peace. Straight ahead, along a well-traveled dirt path, came a young man who carried the Love of the world within his heart. He was known as the prince, and he was about to be married on the following evening. He felt such joy and happiness. He could hardly contain it! Throughout his entire life, he had always been a happy person. He had been given all that he needed and had been born into a family which was rich with love and taught him about the universe and God. He had always had an unusual faith in God, his Loving Creator, and he felt he had been given more than his share of wonderful blessings by Him. Now, he was about to be given the most wonderful gift of his life – a beautiful, tender, loving woman to be his wife. The special evening drew closer. As one could imagine, the wedding was to be a most spectacular event. Many people had traveled great distances to be a part of this joyous occasion. That night, the prince and his beautiful bride saw only each other in their world. Even the beauty of the stars could not compete with the beauty they saw in each other's eyes. They were so much in love.

Many years passed. Their lives together were filled with love and devotion. They gave birth to four beautiful children, who by this time had grown into adolescence. The prince felt his life was complete. One day, after he had been out walking in the back orchards, he came home and opened the door. He felt a chill, a coldness, enter his body. It was only a feeling, but something was about to change, and he knew it. Soon he understood what it was. His beloved wife was no longer there. She had vanished, and no one knew where. It was rumored that she departed with a handsome man whom she had been seen with occasionally. Nevertheless, it was true: she was gone. The prince retreated into his room for many months – seeing no one, not even going out to greet the sun. The light which was once so predominant in his eyes began to fade. Bitterness and anger now began to fester within his heart. That took the place of the overflowing joy and love he had felt before. The bitterness was always close to the surface, and when he began to go out and see people once again, it oozed out and spread. The prince, although he became more outgoing as the years passed, began to truly change. He became a very selfish man, surrounding himself with all the comforts a man could wish for. His world began to center only around himself. He even started being angry at God, for he felt He had somehow caused his misfortune in life and taken away his beloved wife along with all his dreams. It never occurred to him that his youthful dreams might have been selfish.

Soon, his health began to fail. He was stricken by a most paralyzing disease. All his children were gone by now, for they had grown and married, and begun lives of their own. He had never felt so alone in his life. He had no one. His health progressively got worse. Every muscle knew pain. He could not walk unless he had assistance, and even his speech was beginning to slur. There were doctors who tended to his physical needs, but even that could not ease the pain which was felt in his heart as well as his body.

One evening, as he went to sleep, he cried out in anguish and despair to God, "Why me? I was a good husband and father. Why me? I don't deserve this pain! My body is almost gone. You took my dreams. I am nothing. Please take me from this life. Give me Peace." At just the right time, when he was ready, a beautiful gentle Being of Light appeared before his very eyes. This Holy Being held open his arms and spoke softly to him. "My son, why do you not look at the Light? I have known you from the beginning and watched your life unfold. Why do you choose the path of selfishness? You are pre-occupied by your health, by your lost dreams, and by your pain. Yet, inside you know of the Light which you are. You touched Love once, and that was never lost." The prince sat up and argued, "I have forgotten about Love. My life is only suffering. I have no real friends. I have people who obey my wishes and who serve me, but no one comes to me out of Love. I feel there is a hard suit of armor all around me and I cannot get out, nor do I really want to. I am used to loneliness, pain, and emptiness. Look, in spite of my miserable life, I have everything materially a man could ever wish for."

The Being of Light softly replied, "But are you happy? Do you miss knowing the Presence of God? Do you dream of being free from your armor? Do you want to love again?" The prince began to cry. He murmured, "I trusted God all my life. He blessed me with such happiness. I opened to Him and let Him into my life. He led me to Love. And look what happened. I can never trust Him again. I can never Love again. It hurts too much. I do not know if I have the strength to go forward – to turn from my selfish ways and begin to touch the Light again. Oh, I am so frightened."

With a voice that sounded like an angel's the Being of Light replied, "My dear son, come ... come into the Light. Open your Heart. It is never too late to acknowledge who you really are as Light, and to begin to truly Love." The prince stood up and glided over to this Being of Light. They embraced. They were merged into a vibration of Love like the prince had never experienced before. He could not resist. He was only Light, and he knew it. His life became so clear to him. He knew the direction he was now to go. A Peace came over him and he was ready … ready to now be the beautiful, loving, selfless soul he knew he really was. It was true. It is never too late.

Lift Up Thine Eyes

There was a man who walked on this beloved planet two thousand years ago. He spoke of Love. His very life radiated total Love. Some people traveled great distances to sit in His presence and let the vibration of the Word come into their hearts. But many people felt uncomfortable around Him. They remarked to themselves: "Who is this man who would talk of Love and yet make me feel so dirty? This must not be good." And they walked away from him. Then there were those who felt so good about what they heard, and so joyous as they shared a fellowship together. But, when they found they had to change and personally take some serious steps toward that change, they began to experience fear, and they too simply excused themselves and left. Yet, there were also those very, very few who listened, opened their hearts, saw the steps to be made, and welcomed the challenge. They knew somehow that a great opportunity had been offered them through that challenge. They were given the gift to live in the Presence of the One who was sent to teach humanity about the Love God has for his children, as well as to guide them back home. Even those few did not fully understand the meaning of the Love that He talked about, but they felt in their hearts a calling to the Energy which was flowing through the words. This is what kept them going through the changes and the hardships they had to face. There were times they were sent into villages without any provisions whatsoever ... and sometimes even into places where the people did not want to hear their message at all. Above everything else, they were to trust they would be provided for and that God would flow through them as the expression of Divine Love, even during those difficult times. They were to trust they were not alone.

One day, one of the young men was asked to go by himself to a strange place many miles away from where they were all staying at the time. He gladly began his journey. What little he had with him was used up by the third day of his travels. It was scorching hot at that time of the year, and there was not much water to be found. He managed to discover a small bush underneath which he crawled for a few hours in order to be in the shade. Night began to fall. Now he was getting cold. He began to wonder if he would ever see another sunrise. Suddenly, his body jerked awake and he heard someone say, "Where is God now?" He felt so alone. Then horror took over and he started to shake with tears of desperation filling his eyes as other thoughts entered into his mind. What had he done wrong to be out in the wilderness alone and nobody to care for him? If he had only learned more or understood more, maybe he wouldn't be in this predicament now. Surely, he could have done better. He was just not worthy enough to be representing the Light ... yes, that Light which he certainly did not understand. But why didn't God come and comfort him now? Why did he not feel that he was loved by God? "Oh, sweet sound of eternal rest, take my body! There is nothing else to live for. I am abandoned. I am alone!" Such were the sounds that each cell of his body echoed forth in pain.

Just as he was feeling utterly hopeless and consumed by an all-encompassing despair, he perceived something like a shock wave pass through his body. He was startled and woke right up. What happened? He looked at the stars and a strength came into his being. "No more! Oh, my Beloved Father, I reach for Your Heart, and I know You will answer. I am Your Child of Light, and if it be Your Will that I stay in this wilderness, let it be so. I trust you to care for me as you have trusted me with Your Love. I know I am not alone, for You are with me. Yea, You are my every move, my every thought. It is Your Love, Your Light I carry within. May Thy Will be done. I am at peace, for I am Love." At that very moment, he was encompassed in a beautiful shaft of Light. His whole body felt as if it expanded into the outermost reaches of the universe. The overwhelming feeling of inner Divine Joy was almost too much. He felt the presence of the One who had guided and taught him about the Light. There was no resistance ... he just let go. Slowly, he felt he was being gently picked up. That was the last thing he remembered. When he woke up, he was in a cool, grassy, round meadow listening to his beloved Master talking about Love. Sitting beside him were several brothers and sisters of Light. They offered him fresh fruit and nuts. With tears of joy, he accepted the food and offered thanksgiving to God, his Father.

So it was years ago ... the seeds of Love were planted. Those seeds are now ready to blossom. As they blossom, let us be thankful, for we are that much closer to knowing their fruits. As each one of us opens more to God, all of humankind is lifted up. May the strength of His Love sustain all of us as we begin to accept the opportunities offered now and may His Peace be with us all.

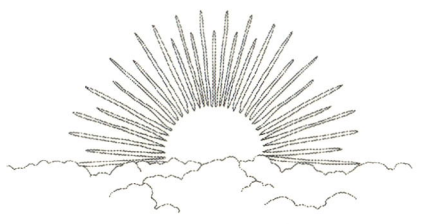

We Are One

There it was again. She could not get the image out of her mind, nor heart. It was so clear. It was as if two very transparent bubbles of Life were floating before her very eyes. It was a bright sunshiny day. The wind was not active. The leaves on the trees were still, as if in a sacred prayer. She looked again and rubbed her eyes. Yes, they were floating, bobbing up and down, as if they had a life of their very own. She began to stare in amazement as they kept coming closer together. Time stood absolutely still. Even the rocks were holding their breath. These giant bubbles, vibrant and alive, touched each other ever so gently and began to dissolve one into the other – oh – so – slowly as if to live the bliss of union for each and every moment. The sun began to get brighter, she thought, as she herself felt touched by this glimpse into Life.

She began to feel very sleepy and sat down under a large oak tree, and began to dream. She imagined herself as one of those bubbles floating freely in outer space. There was such a sense of peace and expansion. Just then she stretched out and became conscious of a change. She observed another bubble of Light exactly like her. She knew they were One. They delighted in the playful, yet sacred union as they dissolved one into the other, each time knowing more about who they were. They called themselves "One-as-Two." They felt such a Love for their Source and for each other that with each blissful explosion of Love, they were sent throughout space to learn, grow, and give.

One day, they found themselves hovering over a beautiful Emerald planet, and once again, being filled with such Love, they merged, knowing and loving the Source of their Being. They then came through the tunnel of Life and appeared on the surface in two forms. There were others around who witnessed this simple, yet direct entrance. Some were frightened, and some seemed to be waiting for their arrival and were grateful. Being Children of the Sun, these "One-as-Two" did not understand the fear demonstrated that day, for they came only to Love and point the way back to freedom and union with the All, God. Many years after their appearance, there came a very sad day. Those who had remained frightened and very suspicious of the "One-as-Two" kidnapped one of the pair and locked her deep within the earth. For seven days the entrance to the "prison" was guarded, day and night.

On the eighth day, just as the sun was about to rise, there was a great Sound heard throughout the entire world. It began very deep and was almost inaudible. It started to rumble until all the elements of creation sang forth in unison, a sound which shattered even the hardest of hearts. Everyone from miles around began to gather by the hole in the earth and hum their heart's song of freedom. Suddenly, in the distance appeared the male aspect of the pair "One-as-Two." He seemed Radiant and shone brilliantly before the rising of the sun. He began to change shape before their very eyes. Lighter and lighter he became. Now straight ahead, emerging from the hole came the one imprisoned. She too appeared like a shimmering Light.

We Are One

They joined hands and spoke to the people: "Gentle children of Light, there is no need to be afraid. We desire nothing of your world. But, there is a world we have come here to share with you. That is our world. It consists only of Love, only of rejoicing in the presence of God, the All in all. It is one whereby you know and live Union. You need no longer to be slaves to the limited thoughts of separation. This world is there for all creation. Lo, it is home to all creation. There we are One, just as here we are One. We must go, for our time here in your world is over for now. We will return some day. As we only see God in the trees that you stand next to, and the water that you drink, and the air you breathe, we see only God radiating through you. Wake up, children of Love. Wake up to your innocence, your purity, your grandeur. There will come a time when you will long to know that Reality and when you will seek only to know God in you. Then call out from the fullness of your hearts and that call will be answered. Peace be with you."

And they all stood motionless as if that moment could have gone on forever if they would have only permitted it. Suddenly, as the "One-as-Two" turned to depart, the Light around them began to expand. It encompassed them fully. It was so bright that many turned their heads away. They got closer and closer together until it was as if they dissolved one into another, and began to float, bobbing up and down. Then they disappeared into the rising sun.

Just then, the wind began to blow and an acorn from the tree bounced joyfully off the girl's head as she was sleeping under the tree. She opened her eyes, and before her stood a young man, extending his hands to her, He merely said, "Come, it is time". She leapt to her feet, placed her hand in his, and remembered. "Yes, we are One. Let us go."

From the Beginning

Once there was a beautiful garden set upon a hill overlooking the earth. It contained the very breath of life: the Light Divine. A pure, radiant ray of Love pulsed forth, straight from the heart of God, touching gently but powerfully upon the garden. Every atom and particle within this garden responded and felt the joy of Love Divine. The earth opened and received this stream of Love straight into her heart, deep within the very core of her Being.

The plant life was lush, fragrant, and magnificent, springing up everywhere in perfect form, balance, and grace. Every shape complemented every other, and they shared life as One … not living off of each other, not needing one another's destruction to survive … but being fed by the Fountain of Life itself, sharing in its everlasting waters of abundance. There was a Sound vibrating constantly within and without, and in that Sound, all knew themselves and God to be One. With every moment of every single breath, each Being knew its Source, each Being followed that call; each Being felt what all Beings felt. What they felt was Joy. There was truly Peace upon the earth.

Sons of Light were sent forth onto the world to tend the garden and to delight in its fruits: both, those of the flesh which grew freely, and fell softly and willingly into the hand that hungered; and those of the Spirit, which flowed freely and without resistance from heart to heart. They set foot upon the garden and felt its beauty, and the commitment in their hearts was true and pure. And Man began, as One. Both, male and female was He.

The rest of the world felt their coming, and something changed forever. Man, the Sons of Light, brought a gift unto the people of the earth – those who lived outside the garden. The gift was like a seed, which needed careful tending and nurturance. Its flower grew in the depths of the soul as perfect love. It was planted in good soil, and the crop began. The gardeners watched over its growth upon this world of time and space.

But something began to happen that they did not expect, (though God had known it would happen from the beginning.) They began to feel the strange sensations of the earth: the tugs, the yearnings, and the pleasures of the body. It was most unusual. They began to feel a strange sort of fascination with these new "feelings", and some sought to explore them more deeply. They did so, in the beginning, in innocence.

Yet, as they began to find themselves drawn to focusing more and more upon the vibrations of the earth, as perceived through their bodies of matter which they wore, they began to notice something else. They could feel more of a difference between themselves – one from another. What had once been only a slight shade of the tiniest difference in vibration between them, now appeared to be an actual distinction between themselves and the others. As they focused more upon their own sensations and experiences, they felt less of one another. And it was odd for them. They began to perceive themselves as individuals – not separate from, but distinct from one another. Yet, they still acknowledged their Source and kept to their sacred mission.

A great Light Being – exceedingly beautiful and powerful to behold – was "in charge" of this garden project. Yet, without the others realizing it, there was a subtle but vitally important difference in his intention in being there. For while the others had never questioned, feared, or doubted God as their Source of Being, <u>this</u> Light Being felt himself to be his own source, and wished for others to recognize this "truth". He sought his own ways, and felt he had a better plan, and knew he could only count on himself.

And through him, the focus of the gardeners was distracted just long enough for another vibration to enter into the world through this holy door that had opened to the touch of God's Love. And this vibration was not of the Light, and it was not of the freedom to Be. And the earth reeled in pain and cried out deep into the night. And her tears filled all the oceans and beyond. Yet not one saw -- or very few -- what it would really mean in the days to come. For though the Light itself was never damaged, tainted, or even diminished, the earth herself and those that lived upon her, did not seem free any longer to live in conscious awareness of that Divine purity that had been expressed since the beginning.

Suddenly those within the garden felt a great shift. And before they even knew it, they felt apart from their Source. And though the Sound continued, it was no longer sweet, for bitterness had added its voice. They cried out, but the Love which they had always felt within their hearts from their very beginning as Souls, was gone. It was lost, and they could not find it. They could not even feel it. And their cry shook the very heavens to their foundations.

The Creator heard, and in His Silence, blessed them for what they would now have to endure, in order that His Kingdom might still come and flourish in fullness upon the world in times to come. Never had His Love left them – never could it leave them. They were His children. If it were possible, He loved them even more now. And so, He took His most precious gift -- His own Beloved Son – wrapped Him in a cloak of matter and sent Him into the world. He sent Him physically (for He had always been there in Spirit) that through His presence and through His life, the world would one day be Free again. Thus, the seed of the Kingdom would grow to full harvest to be shared by all. And life went on for longer than we can measure. Gradually, His promise was being fulfilled.

The Son of Man walks among us again. For this is the day, this is the place, and you are the ones. You are now free to Be in Purity once more, and forever. The Light has come, and the darkness shall be no more. Be happy: no greater Love has ever been shown, even from the beginning. The garden has come again, and from this day forward, the Kingdom has a home on earth. Glory Be to God for ever and ever. His Love has touched the garden, and it has responded. Simply open your heart and Live.

The Promise of the Sun

Once there was a solar system far away in space that had an unusual and special planet. It was special because it had an extremely long elliptical orbit that brought it close to its sun for a very long time, causing the planet's temperatures to rise and its surface to become very beautiful and warm, like a tropical paradise. And as this special planet slowly moved in its orbit away from its sun, the temperatures dropped and the light greatly diminished until only the faint glow of its distant sun could reach it. During this time, which lasted for hundreds of years, all of the large plants, flowers, and trees died from lack of sun. All green life disappeared and the ground became covered with snow and ice. The inhabitants learned to survive on food found in the deep seas which did not completely freeze. People built their homes and roads of snow and ice and wore layer upon layer of clothes for warmth.

It was during one long, Age of Winter when their sun appeared so very faint and distant that the people began to forget about the return of the Light. How this happened no one could tell for certain, but very gradually there was less and less spoken about the "Age of the Sun." People could no longer clearly remember the truths their parents had told them about the Light and the promise of its return. The colors they had heard about in their stories became foreign to them – the blue of the sky and seas, the green of the ground, the incredible things they had called flowers and trees – those things now seemed nothing more than fantastic tales. How could there be anything but the blackness of night, and the pale grays and the dullness of the ice and snow? No one had ever seen anything different. And sadly, almost everyone forgot about the beautiful color and warmth of the Age of the Sun. And, to even dare to speak of such things that might stir the painful memory of those long-forgotten legends, became strictly forbidden.

But quietly, there grew a small group of people who could not forget. To them the legend of the Sun's return was the truth. They could not forget in their hearts the memory of the Light. They would meet in secret and speak of the promise that would one day surely be fulfilled. Whenever this group would try to tell the other people of their joy, their knowing, they were almost always met with great resistance and fear. Many of the "Believers in the Sun," as they came to be called, were hated and treated most cruelly for trying to "misguide" the populace. And yet, the Believers in the Sun and their descendants would never forsake what they knew was true, and they quietly spoke the truth wherever there was an open heart to hear it. "The Sun is coming!" they reminded anyone who had ears to hear. The promise of the Sun was their strength.

Gradually, as the long generations passed, the motion of their planet in space took them past and around the farthest curve of its orbit, and the sun started slowly to grow brighter. No one even noticed it for several years. But, day by day, the Light was increasing and gently changing the planet's surface. As the warmth increased, people suddenly began to notice impossible things. The ice on the sea would sometimes crack when someone walked on it. Water that was free-flowing, and not solidly frozen, was actually seen on the ground. It became warmer, and people were amazed that they could remove an entire layer of clothing, and yet still be warm.

The Sun grew brighter. Many people panicked as they saw their homes begin to turn to slush and water. They cried out in terror as their roadways and settlements of ice and snow disappeared. Some people refused to believe in what was happening, and they remained inside their melting homes of snow and hid from the Light beneath their blankets.

The Believers in the Sun, however, knew the promise was being fulfilled. Who could comprehend such joy? How long they had waited! And now, even though their lives, too, were being greatly disrupted by the changes, they blessed the Creator that this was actually happening in their lifetime. They went out among the frantic people who had so greatly scorned them before, and worked with them, offering them a way out of what seemed to be chaos. The Believers in the Sun once again told the long-forgotten truths about the promise of the Sun's return. Through their service, the fear in many hearts was turned to joy.

Gradually the little seeds that had lain dormant under the cold snow for so very very long, became warmed by the sun and began to sprout. The miracle of the colors returned to the planet. The shining surface of the now liquid sea was a brilliant blue. The land became quickly covered with lush green grasses, plants, and baby trees. The miracle of a flower was beheld by all.

The people rejoiced in the radiant face of the Sun and vowed that never again, throughout any age, would they permit the promise of the Sun to be forgotten.

The seed of God is in us. Given an intelligent and hard-working farmer, it will thrive and grow up to God, whose seed it is; and accordingly its fruits will be God-nature. Pear seeds grow into pear trees, nut seeds into nut trees, and God seed into God.[3]

Meister Eckhart

The Divine Invitation

Mitron and Sharra could not really remember the earliest time they had met these two mysterious Beings that kept appearing in their conscious awareness. It was so very long ago that somehow these two had always seemed part of them – even from the beginning. But one summer day something occurred that they really saw as a gift to them from their eternal friends of long ago.

It was a warm, sunny day, not unlike any other day. Mitron and Sharra were young and had been playing in a nearby meadow. As young children do, they had spent their afternoon running, climbing trees and gazing into the clouds. Mitron had just stopped for a second to catch his breath while Sharra continued to play tag with the butterflies as they delighted in chasing after her for a change. Sharra glanced over to Mitron. He seemed to be lost somewhere in his thoughts. He was spellbound, looking upwards. She went over to him and sat beside him. Suddenly, she was aware of what he was seeing. It was a great silver disc in the sky which seemed to be hovering right above them. A single beam of light came from the center of the disc and extended down to touch the earth only feet from where they were sitting. Startled, they jumped up and felt very excited. They knew something wondrous was about to occur.

They kept their eyes glued on the column of Light. Two Beings of Light began to descend down the center of the column until they were standing right in front of Mitron and Sharra. The two children felt like they were greeting two very special friends they had known forever but hadn't seen in a very long time.

Without hesitation, both of the youngsters glided into the column to embrace their friends, and in an instant they were lifted into the great silver disc. Just as they began to look around they felt themselves losing conscious awareness of their surroundings. When they awoke they were looking at a huge screen. There hovering in space was a beautiful planet, virgin in its expression, yet full with all forms of life yearning to know more of their maker, their creator. They could feel this pristine beauty as they came closer to the planet. They found themselves lost in the scenes they were seeing.

All at once, they realized they were no longer watching a screen as they had been. Instead, they found themselves on a small spaceship circling this very same planet. Somehow they knew everything was in order and they communicated the thoughts to each other that they would keep on going no matter what happened. They would just let go and allow themselves to be shown what they were there for. So, they slowly approached the planet feeling that this was not the first time they had visited this emerald jewel. They saw such diverse expressions of life forms, such as brilliant colored birds, broad-leafed lush green forests with mist rising from below, giving the impression of a newly-formed creation. Mitron and Sharra were filled with a sense of peace as they observed nature expressing such harmony and union. What a beginning!

Suddenly, their ship seemed to enter a tunnel, as if controlled by some outside source. Again they both lost conscious awareness of their environment. They seemed to float endlessly about in the narrowness of this space. Eventually, they found themselves emerging from the tunnel. They were first blinded by the brilliance of the Light. Once they got their bearings, they saw they were at the very same spot where they seemed to have blanked out. But the time seemed to have advanced so much! They could see the planet below. They both felt an uneasiness overtake them as they looked closer. What was it that was so different?

They felt they were to go even closer still. What they saw astonished them. The pristine beauty and life seemed to be gone. They observed whole communities of people who seemed to be so frightened. Why?

Somehow, they felt they were to go even closer. Instantly they found themselves walking on this emerald planet, wondering how they had gotten there, yet still knowing everything was in Divine order. They began to mingle with the people from the village. They kept hearing them talk of a time when they all were living a life of joy and love, where kindness and caring for one another were natural expressions of life. There seemed to be a deep longing for those times. That was truly evident in the voices of the people they talked with. What happened? Sharra and Mitron really wanted to know, for what they saw the people were living was only loneliness, fear, and total separation.

For days, the two of them spent all their time listening to the stories of the "old ones". It had happened all so suddenly they were told. It was like this: One moment the village was singing for the Glory of God, with One voice. The sweetness of their song carried for miles around. They were happy for they sang of the presence of God their creator. All nature joined in the song.

Then one day, a young man appeared at the village gate. He was a tall and attractive sort of a fellow, with an aura of self-confidence about him. He had a beautiful voice – one that as he sang all would listen. Everyone was captivated by the sound which came from him. He sang of the glories of Heaven. He sang of Love. But something began to feel all so wrong, so empty. More and more people followed him and there began to be two voices now. Suddenly, people began to see each other differently. Some were delighted with how wonderful they were feeling. Finally they were receiving recognition for their skills. At last, they were becoming somebody. Many were confused and frightened. A few were overcome with a deep sadness. Who are we serving? Ourselves? This Stranger? God? What have we done? Even at that time, those few rare ones still felt it was "we" even if they didn't participate in the act of separation. They just longed for the conscious Oneness to return in total manifestation.

After hearing about and feeling the pain within all the people's hearts, it was nearing the time for Mitron and Sharra to depart from the village. It was then that they began to get a funny feeling all over their bodies. What they saw was remarkable. Just above the village, as if in mid-air, were their two "timeless" friends. They were radiant and so full of Love. They began to speak. "We are all free Beings of Light. It is time now to return to the true knowing of our One voice. It is the same voice that sounds forth through all creation. It is changeless. None of us receives any recognition for ourselves as it flows through. It is Divine. Are we ready to accept to allow God to be God in us? Are we ready to let go of the error of perception that we can get something out of being separate from one another, from God? We do not have to live this way anymore. We can know of our true Oneness, right now! Extend your hearts to one another. Open up and let go. Be One." Everyone was spellbound, especially Mitron and Sharra. It was as if a Light which was beyond any description filled everyone and everything. There was not one person in that village who was not touched by this divine invitation to know Light, God. Would they respond?

Mitron and Sharra looked at each other and drew closer and closer. All fear, doubt, thoughts of separation disappeared. They were absorbed, one into another, into a sea of Light, an eternal presence of Love. All was in Divine order. They knew they were One. They suddenly felt so free!

Gazing around, they didn't see the village anymore. They were standing under the same tree looking up as a great silver disc departed. All they could say was "Thank you, dear friends, Thank you."

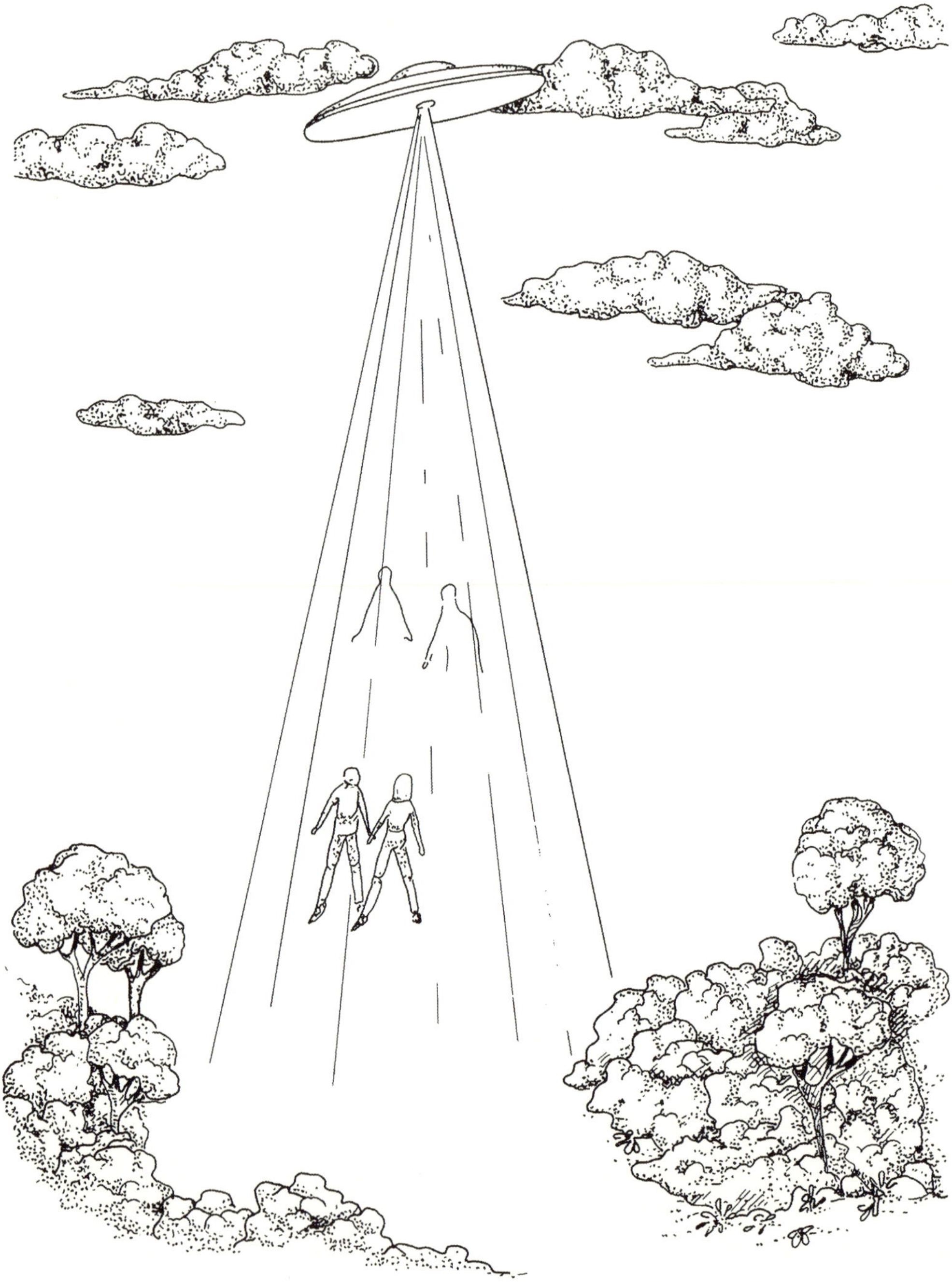

Passion for the Divine

Since the beginning of time, there has always been an ache, a cry from deep within, that beckons us to follow the call to ultimate Union with All that is Real, to merge with God, Our Heavenly Father. The cry does not go away, especially when we begin to pay attention and follow its gentle guidance. It leads us to the threshold of a door that unlocks the greatest mysteries within, secrets kept so deep that we were not even aware they were there. Love is the key that unlocks the door. It is a Love that could only be tasted as we thirst for and desire that perfect Union between ourselves and our Creator, God. It is a Love which activates the original beauty and goodness of our very Soul. The desire to know the world of Spirit while we are still inhabiting a body form becomes so overpoweringly intense that we thrill at the thought that each moment is filled with an opportunity to just glimpse a shadow of the face of God. Each day is permeated with the audible prayer to be free, free from all the distractions which have kept us prisoner of our own created world.

Throughout this planet's history all the great mystics, sages, and masters have quietly urged humanity to let go of the bondage of this world of form and seek only to dwell in the freedom of the world of Spirit and to merge with that ever-present energy of Love. This is Reality to a child of God. We merely need to let go of attachment to our self-centeredness, for there is a greater way to live, a way that shines forth naturally in all of creation. It is the way of God, filled with the gentle and caring touch of the Mother and the universal, unconditional Love of the Father. It is a way whereby we know all Beings on the planet as our brothers and sisters and respect all life forms, for they are the very essence of God, just as we are. We are One, truly. We cannot settle for any lesser way of living, for it would be untruthful. We stand ready to be so totally consumed by the Love for God that literally, all our selfishness and attachments are melted by the divine power of that Love. This vision lies deep within us all, waiting for the time of its awakening.

What does it matter what color we are, what religion we practice or into what nation we are born? We are all children of God. Lo, we are the very essence of God Himself. It is time, now, to open to the manifestation of Union, to reclaim our divine heritage, to live Heaven on earth. We all dream of a time when Love is the only way of life, where caring for others comes before thoughts about ourselves and when loving God with all our heart and soul is our only focus.

Our hearts weep silently at the apparent selfish ignorance of humanity, but at the same time, they rejoice, for that humanity is also ours, and we will not rest until all Beings know of the all-consuming Passion for the Divine, and we are free once more to Love. We are like the young humpback whale who was hopelessly caught in the warm waters of San Francisco Bay and was unable to find an exit and release from her plight. We, like her, will also be lured home, into that unending ocean of bliss by the very sound of our own cry, a deep, passionate cry for the Divine. It will gently lead us deeper and deeper in conscious awareness, into the state of Union with All, with God. There is no other way. Let us follow that call Home, for therein lies our only true joy.

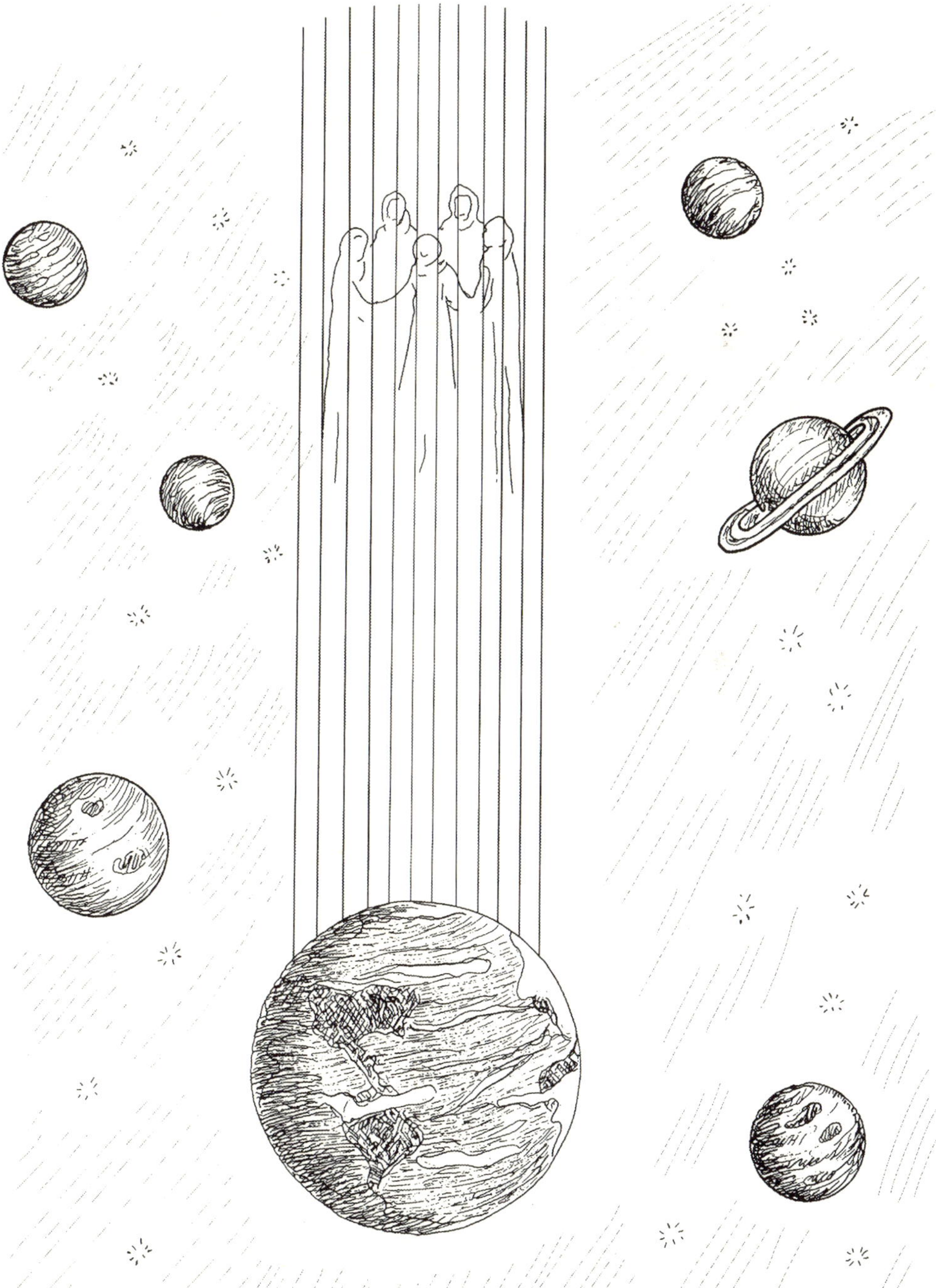

Inside There is a Light

The Son was shining through all creation. The birds were singing a song of joy as the trees bowed to all nature. Life was renewed. The air was alive with the breath of Light. Underneath one of the trees was a tiny little girl with wispy golden curls that fell below her shoulders. She was curled up in a ball, holding her knees to her chest. Her cheeks were moist with soft tears that gently rolled down her face. Yet, she wasn't sad – just very, very much alone. The branch of the tree bent down and touched her head. It really wanted to pick her up, if only it could … but it knew it shouldn't interfere. The little girl looked up as she heard the words, "Little Angel of Light, why do you weep?" She thought for a moment, dried her eyes, and said, "I am so afraid. I am so alone. Maybe he'll never come back." The tree sighed for it knew of her pain. It gently replied, "Maybe you are not looking in the right place for your Beloved Father. You've been looking up the rocky paths, into the skies, and around my body, thinking he might be hiding in one of those spots. Do you not know you cannot find Him in anything outside of you if you haven't seen Him inside of you first?" The little girl looked confused, but somehow she felt better. She was now ready to let go of the shade and comfort of the tree and begin to walk the path Home. Her steps were brisk and her pace was determined. All went smoothly until the night started to settle in all around her. The sounds of the forest began to overtake her and she found herself getting frightened again. She felt so very vulnerable, so bare as if she was totally unprotected from all those unknown nightly elements. She was so alone. Why didn't her Father come and deliver her from this forest of darkness? The sounds got louder, and the trees seemed as if they were leaning in. She was getting scratched by the thorns on the bushes. The forest path was getting so thick, she wondered if she could take one more step ahead. She couldn't help herself. She started to cry. Her little blond curls were all snarled and twigs had snagged themselves in her hair. "Oh Father, if you love me, come rescue me now from this place. I am so scared. Why don't you hear me? Where are you? I thought you loved me. Why do you make me so afraid?" Immediately, she felt gentle droplets of water falling on her skin, like dew drops from heaven. The path began to open up as a large Bird of Light descended upon her. She was gently lifted up, way up into the air, over the treetops and far, far away. They flew for a long time until they reached a crystal clear mountain which seemed higher than any other mountain around. A small passageway into this beautiful mountain opened up as they came closer. As they went inside they were immediately surrounded by a warmth that seemed to come from the brightness of the Light all around them. The little girl fell down and wept, even though she did not know why she was crying, for there was not one part of her that was not total joy. The days ahead were filled with happiness she had not felt in a long time.

It seemed like they stayed in that mountain room forever. Everything was wonderful until one day the beautiful Bird of Light came to the little girl and said, "Little One, today is the day I must leave and go away. You must remember why you are here. You were brought here in your search for your Father. It is while you are here that you may find Him. Remember what you were told. You must find Him within yourself first before you will ever see Him outside of you in any of the outer forms in the world. This is a time for you to truly seek and then to find." The Bird of Light had a gentle loving smile on its face. However, the little girl began to panic. She stuttered and said in a desperate voice, "But wait! Where do I look? Where is the Father inside of me? How do I know when I have found Him? Please, I know what you say is true. I have nowhere else to go, nowhere else to look. I have been everywhere else. But, I am scared. What if He is not there? Oh, stay with me, don't leave!" The Bird of Light softly replied, "Do not be afraid. You will know the Father by the Love you will feel inside your heart." With that, the mountain passageway opened up, and the Bird of Light flew outside and disappeared. The little girl looked around. The only thing she saw was emptiness all about her. Then she sat down and started to think. Inside of her is her Father. Oh, He is so very close. So, she began to tightly squeeze her eyes shut. She had to find out for sure ... and, she had reached the point where she had nowhere else to go. She began to relax and turn her eyes inward. It was sure dark in there. She kept calling out for her Father to show Himself. As she continued to let go, she felt she was being drawn more inside, until the darkness began to turn to light ... and there in the center, was this pulsating ball of Pure Light. She found herself crying and smiling at the same time as she went deeper, right into the very center of that Light. It was as if the days of yesterday, those of tomorrow and that very instant were all the same, as she spun around faster and faster. She kept feeling as if she was going to explode at any moment. Was this her Father? Then she remembered what the Bird of Light had said about knowing her Father by the Love she would feel in her heart. Just as she thought about that, something happened. It seemed like her whole world opened up. She burst forth and experienced a Love she had never dreamed existed. Her world became that vibration of Love ... Pure and Divine ... a tone which hummed through every cell of her body. She was carried deeper into that sound until she became the very sound of Love itself. At that moment, she knew she was never to be apart from her Father again. She and her Father were One ... they always were and always would be One. How magnificent and glorious was that Light within!

The next thing she remembered was once more being carried by the Bird of Light and flying over the treetops until they reached a small familiar village. However, she found that everything looked slightly different. As she was gently put down on the ground, she turned around and looked in all directions. She was amazed as she started to behold a beautiful Light inside of everything she saw. She recognized this Light as being the same Light she had experienced living inside of her. Inwardly, she smiled, for she had finally understood. She felt so good. She had found her Father ... He had never left. She had just forgotten for a moment where He was. How could she ever have not trusted Him to love her and care for her? But now that she knew the truth, she would never doubt Him again. She was home to stay.

And so it was. The Son continued to softly hum a song of Love. And a gentle peace filled the hearts of all living things.

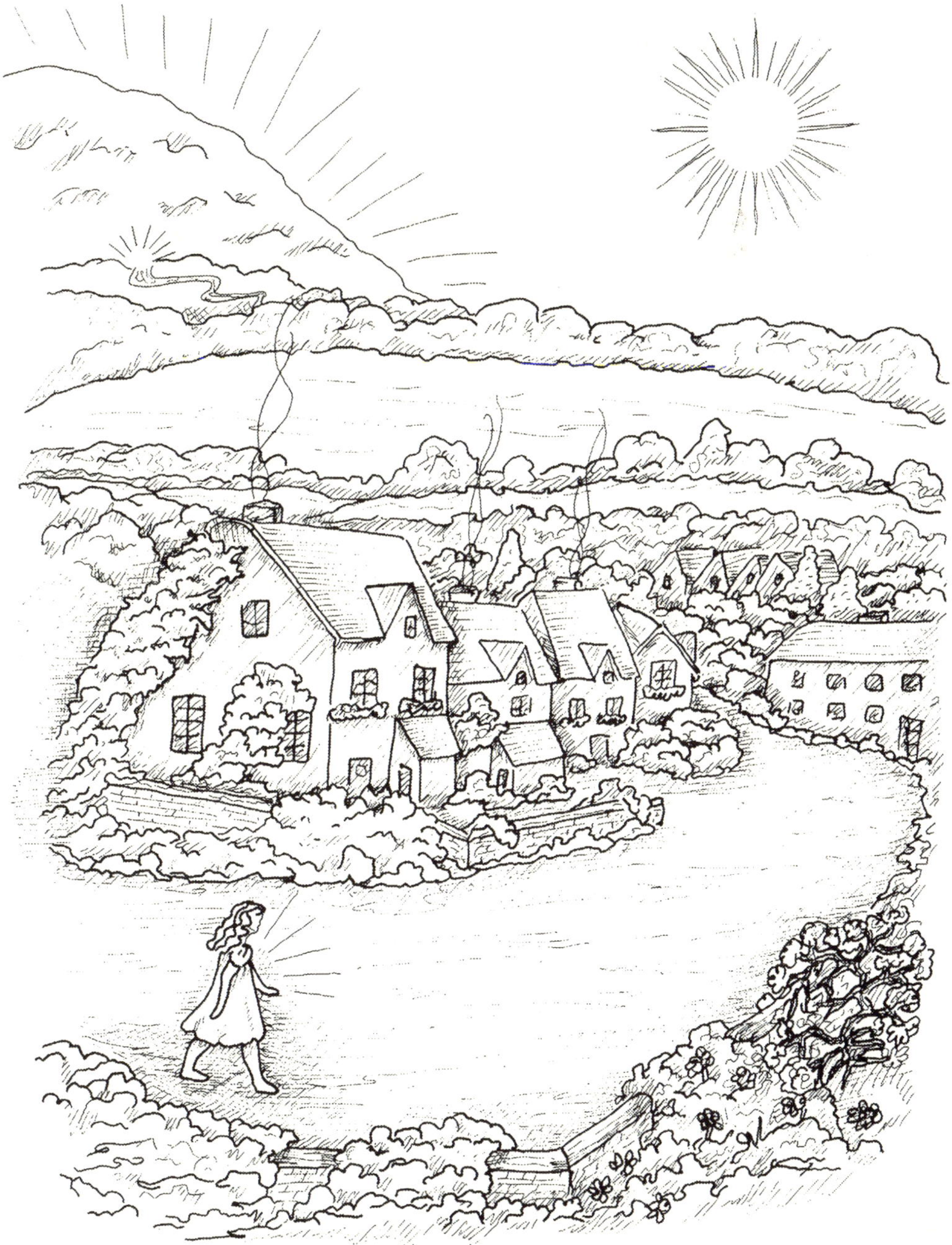

The Smile of the Sun

It was one of those perfectly glorious days, sunny, warm, and glistening with beauty. Birds were singing a most incredible song and the trees were dancing to their song without missing a beat. Yet, at the far end of the forest sat a young girl huddled up into herself, and sobbing a most painful cry. Her little heart was heaving up and down and she felt so lost. She did not hear the song of the birds, nor see the leaves of the trees dancing, even though they came quite close to her head. She did not know why she was so utterly without hope. Yesterday, she was playing with her friends and they were all having such a great time, as young girls have. She remembered that at one point that morning she looked at all of them, and she did not know any of them. They were strangers to her! They all had their dolls and everything else that would make them happy. But she had looked at them and then at herself and she had felt a coldness overtake her. She had begun to shake, even on the outside. It seemed like all the joy and happiness had oozed out of her body. She remembered going home, seeing her family, the house, the cars … She could not connect with any of it. "Oh, God, why am I here?", she cried. Then, she ran out to the forest, her haven, and sat below her favorite tree. "Why? Why? What am I looking for?" she muttered into her knees. So, here she was, cold and alone.

Now, as she sat below her tree, there appeared two gentle souls right before her very eyes. She was startled back to life as she stared at them. Somehow, they were a key to a door within, and she knew it. They let her empty herself fully and then invited her to stand. They took her hands and led her deeper into the forest, places where she dared not ever go for fear of what she might find. But now, for the first time, she felt she could pass by those images which she had kept with her for so long. She entered deeper into the forest until she could not even feel those two radiant Beings of Light anywhere around. With a gentle determination, she stood, straight and tall, closed her eyes and imagined they were still there. Slowly she began to feel the warmth and glow of their presence surrounding her. She knew their love was real and it was truly touching her deep within herself. In a flash, within the center of her head she saw the radiant Sun, so bright, extending outwards throughout all creation. Now deep within the forest, she heard strange and compelling voices, coming from everywhere all at once. She took her eyes off the Sun which she knew animated all things and she instantly felt herself surrounded by a cloak of words, just words – but so thick, so cold, so dense. Her heart became very heavy. She fell to the damp ground, not knowing if she wanted to live another moment. "Sun where are you?" she heard herself yell. Now, where did those particular words come from? Was that her own question, her own thought? Instantly, she felt a strength come over her, both from without and from within. "Oh God, my God, please release me from all that is not real," she shouted. She stood as tall as a giant, eyes closed, and called out with every fiber of her being to know and be united with the Sun once more. She felt herself spinning, over and under as if through a great tunnel of Light. Then a door suddenly opened…

"Could you pass me the butter, please", she heard. She couldn't believe her ears. What happened? She seemed so much older now and she was sitting at a large table, surrounded by friends. She looked around and what she saw made her tremble with Love for God. There was her beloved Sun, smiling back at her through each friend, through the butter, through the cat, through the fish and through herself. She squinted her eyes and looked real hard in the direction beyond the table. She thought she even saw those two gentle souls of Love with such smiles of radiance that they seemed to Light up the whole room. "Now you know. Live the Truth with the passion of Divine Love, for the glory of God. You are never alone. So be it. Peace. Peace. Peace." Then they were absorbed into the brilliance of the Sun

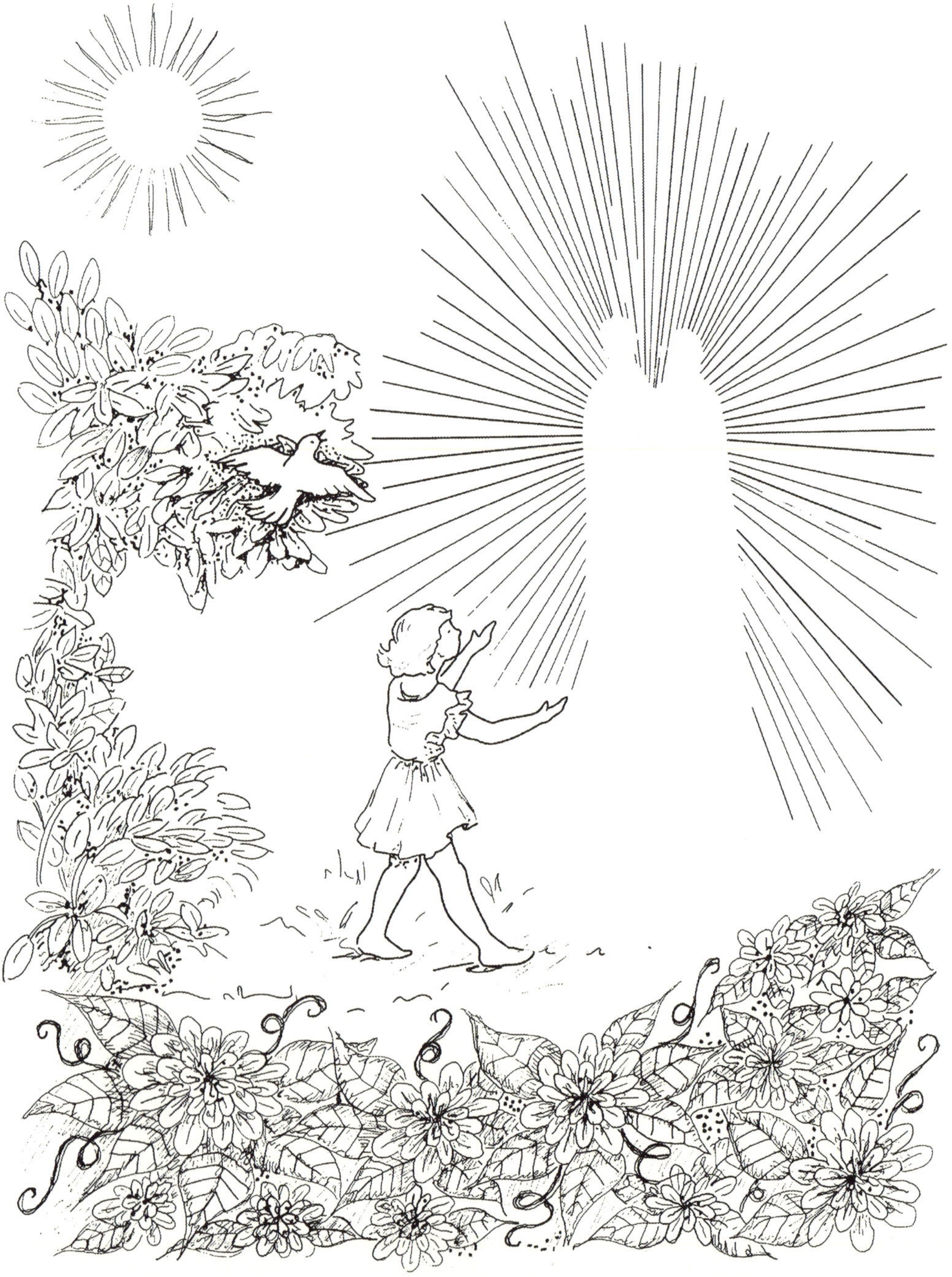

For One Soul

And so it is throughout the life of this beautiful planet called Earth, that there are sent those Beings who have been prepared to carry out the job of representing the Light in its fullest Purity and to let The Christ shine forth unto all Mankind. Along with The Christ come the "wayshowers", the silent workers who help prepare those who are asking to answer that burning call inside -- the call which cries out from their very depths: "I am ready to come Home, to be set free, to love all as God Loves All, to be the LIGHT." The wayshowers keep pointing the way, not to a person or a thing, but straight to God Our Heavenly Father, saying softly, at the same time: "Don't forget to look within, to let go, and let God live His life through you. May Peace be with you on your journey."

So it goes throughout history. Two thousand years ago, one might have seen that gentle man of love who was called Jesus walking in a field, looking and listening inside for that constant guidance from His Father. As the story goes, He had just finished visiting a small village where there used to be many who asked for help which flowed through Him. In the beginning, they had sent forth a plea to be set free, to come Home again. Even thus, the villagers had many secret dreams and expectations about what and where Home was, and how to get there. They also thought they had a pretty good idea about Love. Jesus had been periodically visiting the village during the past years. At first many had listened, and were even excited, for they felt something stirring inside – a yearning for a Life which was pure and simple, and directed solely from the Center of their Beings -- the Same Source, God, that directed the Life flow of Jesus. They were attracted to the same happiness and inner peace they saw that Jesus had, and they wanted to claim it for themselves. It was going well until they had a look deep inside. Then all those inner questions arose. Did every part of their life reflect the Light? Did they manifest and nurture angry and jealous thoughts? Did they really love their neighbors, and not judge them? Was their mental attitude one that was pure, or did they have adulterous relationships in their minds? Were they able to let go of their desires and dreams so they could truly be free, or did they cling fast to even the tiniest of dreams, hoping they would be fulfilled in their own way? Some of the people felt they had gone far enough along the path, as those questions didn't go away. As a result, they chose a life of outer comfort and did not want to look any deeper. Some made lots of excuses and thought this Man, Jesus could never represent Love if he brought pain amongst them. They thought maybe he just wanted their money or possessions and that there must be a catch somewhere. Nevertheless, there were a few who wanted to go further, not knowing even where it was going to take them. But they were willing to go for they knew the Truth was unending. However, each time Jesus returned to this village, there were fewer and fewer people who asked to see Him and who were truly ready to listen with their hearts to what flowed through Him, and then to take responsibility in their own lives for what they were beginning to know as Truth.

So there He was, walking in a field of tall swaying grass, asking His Father, "What do I do? Why did you send me here if you knew that only the very few would listen? Have I done enough?" And His answer came softly from within. "My Son, as long as One Soul on this planet wishes to transcend human personality and limitations and come back Home to Me, You are to stay there and help, thereby letting Me Love through You. My work is Your work. We are ONE." Once again, all those who had been sent to the earth to help with the work of the Christ, promised to remain and continue to do what was being asked of them, day by day, step by step, as it was directed by God.

Several years passed until all was done that could be completed through those means. The time was right to leave. A soft tear rolled down the cheeks of many, as a loving smile was seen on the face of Jesus when He lifted His eyes to His Father. The words uttered in compassion were felt by all living things on earth. *"Father, forgive them, for they know not what they do." (Luke 23:34 KJV)*[4] Such a Love poured forth throughout the Earth at that moment, that even the minerals vibrated and knew they were someday going to also be set free into total Light. Instantly, it was known by all that the Christ would someday return, when humankind and the world was ready to take another step closer to the Heart of God, when they would accept to let go and soar into true Liberation, and when there would be those willing to sincerely live and assume responsibility for what they knew to be True. That day has come. Are we ready? As long as one Soul truly cries out to know the Light, there is hope for humankind and the very Earth itself.

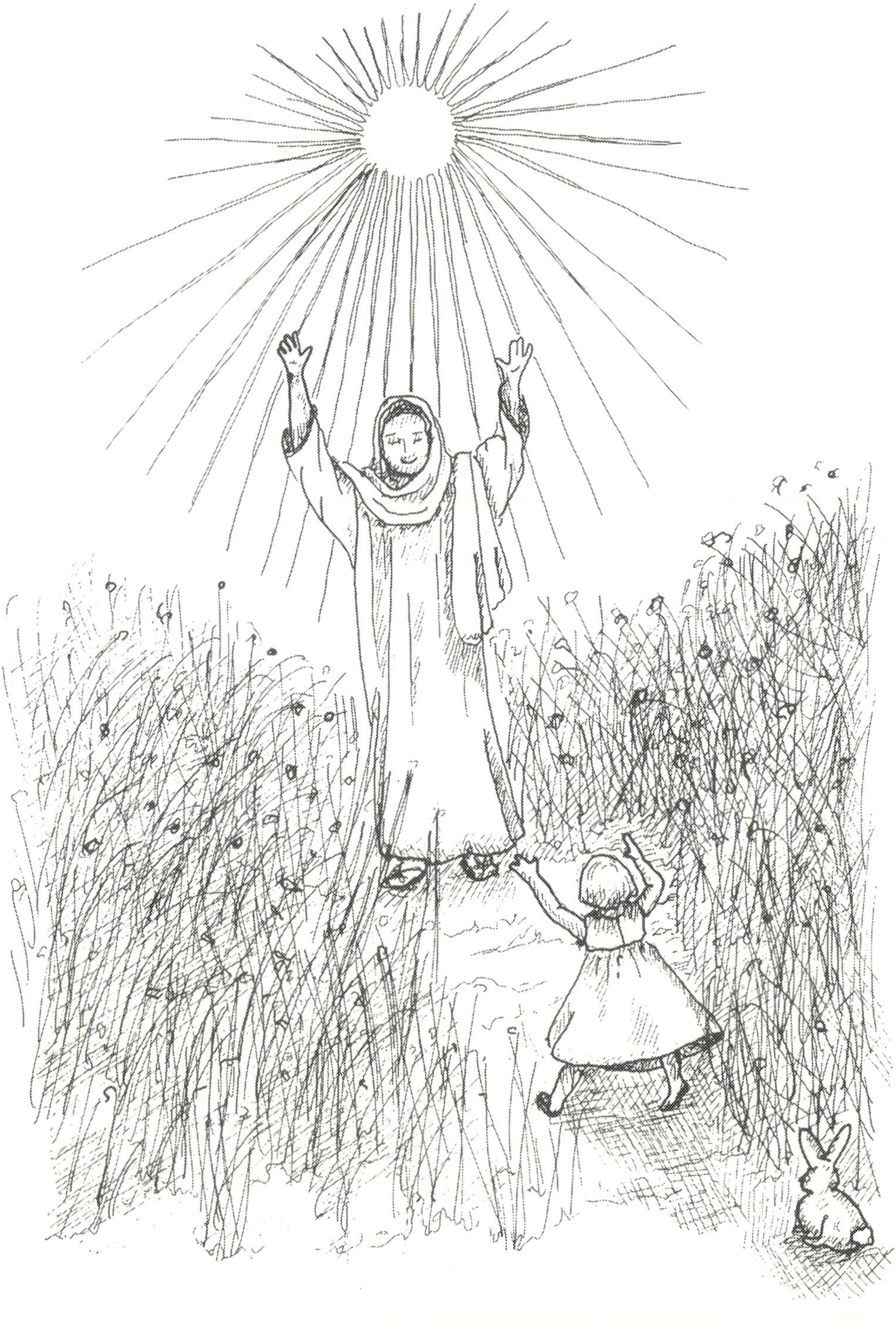

The Promised Land

It was a clear, sunshiny day. The birds were singing and the air was, oh, so warm. A beautiful young girl was strolling through a thickly wooded area. The trees were reaching for the sun and their leaves were vibrating to the Sound of the universe. She paused for a moment to thank them for giving so freely to her ... giving her part of the very source of her breath. She knew how they were One ... One in nature – One in life – One in God. She knew ... One. A bright, radiant light began to come forth through her Heart and gently encircled each tree, softly kissing them, one at a time, with Love. The trees bowed and smiled a "knowing" smile. She walked a little farther, deeper into the forest until she saw a rock. She climbed onto it and sat on the very top. Her eyes got very heavy and finally closed. The Light of the Sun picked her up and held her in His arms. She began to "dream".

What she saw was magnificent. All life, all creatures great and small, sang out together in harmony. She saw all life forms become lighter as their Hearts burst forth in twinkly vortices of Love. They touched one another and merged. Oh, such blending of the universe. "Such Love is unimaginable! Such harmony – can we truly sing that One note of Love?" Her body went limp as she now lay flat upon the top of the rock. She saw a lion and a small lamb frolicking in a meadow, laughing and playing together. That wasn't a fairy tale. There they were, loving each other. She saw a hand of Light descend upon the Earth and caress it, and the Earth responded with a dance of Light. All was changed. It was so much more intensified. The tone was clearer, purer. "Oh, Father, let me know more," she cried out.

Slowly, she woke up from her slumber in the arms of the Sun. He gently put her down in a small clearing, which was close to the forest of Life. When her eyes were fully open and she was awake, she found herself standing by a huge pillar of Light. It seemed to come from beyond the Beyond and it went straight into the very depths of the earth. She felt if she got too close, she might be pulled inside and never come out again. Her heart began to respond to the column of Light, and she had no fear or doubts any longer. She pressed her hands on the Light and found herself in the very center of the Emerald Ray of Vibrant Light. At this moment, all that she thought about, breathed for, and cried out for was the Beloved Son ... and the response was instant. Peace flooded her being. She was not only held in His arms forever; she became the very arms herself. She knew the Son as herself, as He whispered to her: "Dear Soul of Love, I am Light as you are Light. We are One in God's arms, for His arms are my arms. It is He who has comforted you and Loved you forever, and even after that. My dear Angel of Light, You are Love. Go in Peace. Live what you know to be the Truth. May you know God is always in your heart. May you honor that knowing above all else. Peace. Peace. Peace." She knew that the moment she had just experienced within her heart would last until eternity.

The next thing she knew, she heard a delightful, sweet meow, for she had just rolled over on her fluffy little kitten who had come to rest in her bed. She looked at her clock. It was 5:05 AM. Time to get up and begin her day. But she felt different ... she knew that from this moment on, her days would never be the same.

Today, there are those who, in their hearts, have walked with that very same beautiful young girl. They have paused and seen Life lived in true harmony and Love. They have welcomed the Son and His Father into their hearts. They know there is a place to live the Kingdom of God, to BE the Light totally, and to Glorify the name of God in all that is done. They, too, cry out for ultimate freedom, and to know the Truth of God's Love. And like the girl, as their hearts continue to open, they will surely know All.

Prayer of St Francis

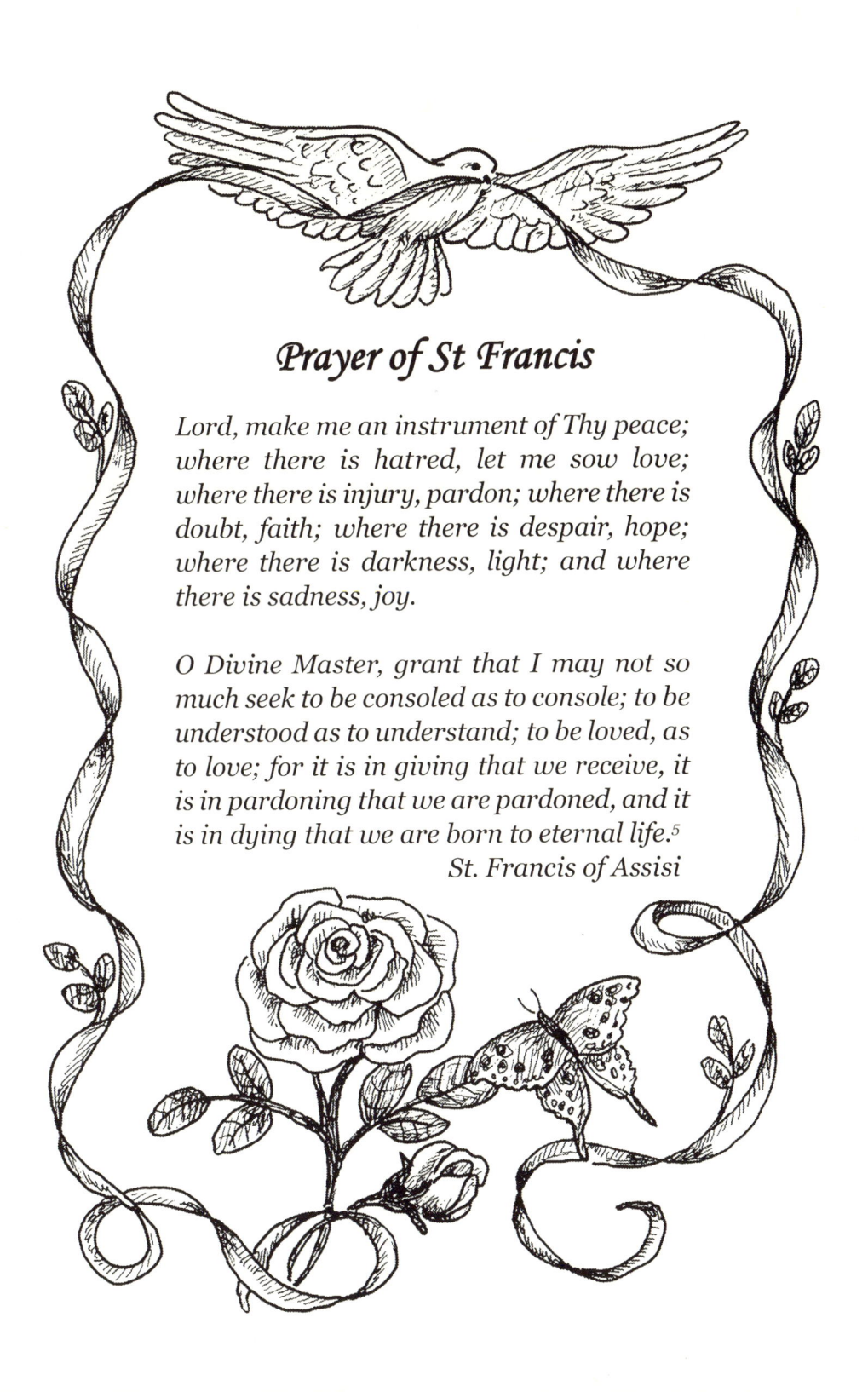

Lord, make me an instrument of Thy peace; where there is hatred, let me sow love; where there is injury, pardon; where there is doubt, faith; where there is despair, hope; where there is darkness, light; and where there is sadness, joy.

O Divine Master, grant that I may not so much seek to be consoled as to console; to be understood as to understand; to be loved, as to love; for it is in giving that we receive, it is in pardoning that we are pardoned, and it is in dying that we are born to eternal life.[5]
St. Francis of Assisi

Home is Where the Heart is

The stars were twinkling in a most playful way. It was truly a magical night. Zephir and Sashelle were sitting by a campfire listening to two radiant beings who were talking as if they were in another world. The words were soft, yet were spoken directly to the heart, "We were only young children at the time, but we can remember it just as if it happened yesterday," they said. They continued their story as they gazed into the dancing fire light.

It was a cool summer morning. The flowers emitted a special sweet fragrance which seemed to fill the air. The sound of the birds singing seemed to ring forth only one sound. Suddenly, for just a moment, all life was frozen. There was no movement, no time. Everything was motionless and all sound had ceased. It was like the earth holding her breath. One minute we were standing in a meadow in the fresh air, and in the next minute we were walking down a path for quite a while until we entered into a valley. We observed how everything we saw had such a golden aura around it, almost transparent. We came to an entrance, like a gateway, which led to a small "village" nestled within the heart of this radiant valley and were then invited into one of the taller buildings. The entire "village" was like a large campus, a living school. We were told that many beings came here from a variety of different locations to learn about their Creator, God. We both could feel this place was part of home to us. Not only were the beings and the school familiar, but so was the life they were living. This was the very same quest we were obsessed with from the very beginning of our lives.

We found ourselves both at awe and, at the same time, filled with excitement. Two very gentle beings came towards us and invited us to go into a beautiful garden. We followed, yearning to know more. Why were we brought here? Were we going to get to stay? Would we ever return to our "other" life, wherever it was? All those questions were present as we sat down in the soft grass on top of a small hill in the center of the garden. The two beings, as if reading our thoughts, answered with eternal patience and genuine kindness, "Little Ones, you are brought here for one purpose: to instill within your memory a vision of your home. Look within and see that all beings here are seeking the same thing, to know God. And yet it is a most unselfish quest. For the exact moment that one of the beings here discovers something more about what is real, that discovery and knowledge is instantly transferred to all. Everyone has a unique aspect of God-nature to express, but yet it is not for their own gain or return. In expressing that pure essence of God, that would glorify God and thus inspire that which is universal, unchanging, timeless, and real in all to be manifested to a greater degree than ever before. Thus this entire expression of life continues to grow in its pure manifestation of God-nature. No one receives any identity or success from any of their actions. Here, all beings continuously open more and more to allow God to express the fullness of His Love through them, for that is their only nature. Therefore, they desire only that pure expression of God to be lived through them. Oh, what freedom lies ahead for you, little ones! But you must trust your hearts and let go. Live for the glory of God. Allow Him to be the doer within you. Don't look back. Just continue to seek courageously, even if no one else seems to be there. You are never alone.

With those words, the two gentle beings seemed to shimmer at such a high vibratory rate that they disappeared from our very eyes, but never from our hearts. We both looked at each other and for one of the first times that we could remember, we saw each other before the beginning. We knew this entire experience was an important event that was given to us. We vowed then and there to always remember those two gentle beings who helped us to remember home and to recognize the very quest of our heart.

… The fire started to sputter and spurt. Zephir and Sashelle jumped as they realized they were still sitting by the campfire. Their parents were calling out their names. Still spellbound, they stood up to yell back to them that they were coming home. When they turned back to the fire to say goodnight to their new friends, they couldn't see them anywhere. Zephir and Sashelle stood motionless as they heard these same words at the very same time, "Yes little ones, you are coming home. It is true. We will meet again." Hearing those words, they were both filled with such a sense of joy. And so, they began their journey home, fully awake … one glorious step at a time.

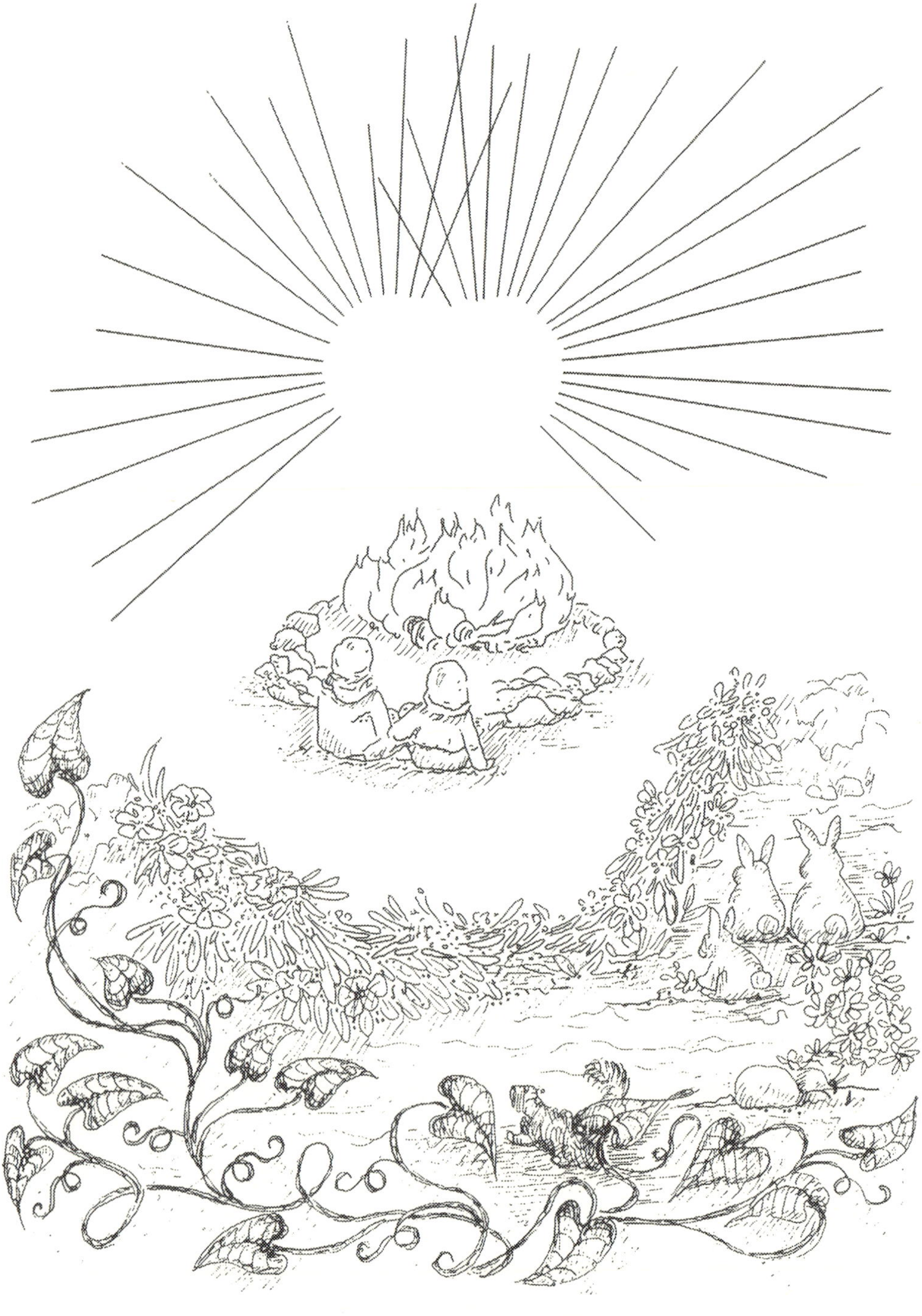

Homeward Bound

Once upon a time, in a land far away, there lived a wise king and his beautiful queen, who was pregnant with their first child. On a glorious, sunny spring day, a gentle baby boy was delivered unto them. They knew, however, their child was not theirs to bring up. So, they sent him with the nursemaid to a very simple peasant family, to be raised, nurtured, and cared for.

The years went by and suddenly everyone in the kingdom could feel something was going to happen. It was time! The king sent a messenger to the peasant family. They were waiting for him, as they knew the day would come when "their" son would have to accept his heritage and begin to rule his royal kingdom. All those years his birthright had been kept a secret. Now the story was out, and the prince was to be given a couple of weeks to accept willingly and freely who he really was. No one would interfere with his decision. However, all the help would be there if he needed it.

At first, this was such a shock to the young prince that when he was told of his "real" parents, he would not even accept the possibility of it being true. Instead, he ran away – far away, so he did not have to hear the words that his beloved peasant parents told him. Three days later, when he returned, he fell into a deep confusion. He tried to forget what he had heard. Simultaneously, he felt both joy and frustration, as well as an attraction and repulsion. But, mostly he felt deceived as if his whole life had been lived as a lie and out of his control. Sadness crept in. it was a sadness of unexplainable proportions, for he was hearing the sound of his own death-cry and his plea for help. Then came the fear. It gripped him so tightly and was so paralyzing that he could not walk or even talk for days. Fear was always there. It appeared every time he would begin to think, "What if this is true if I really am to be the king. I don't know anything about how to be a king. I can't do it. I don't know or understand enough. I feel so alone. It's going to be so hard." He would then cry and cry and cry. Those days of fear began to get calmer until anger overshadowed everything he touched. He thought about all those years and how he could have used them to learn how to be a true king. Instead, his "real" parents sent him to live with a peasant family, where he only learned how to milk cows and work in the fields. What a waste. He began to resent everyone around him until one day, as he was stomping through the forest he stumbled on a root of an old oak tree and fell with a thud on the ground. As he was lying very still and in great pain, both inner and outer, a beautiful emerald green Light came down and engulfed him. His heart began to open and it even skipped a few beats. In one instant, he began to understand everything. His "real" parents loved him so much that they let him go to learn firsthand about the people in his kingdom. He knew in every cell of his body that Love was everything and that his life was in perfect order. He was not alone, and he certainly had everything he needed to become a king. The experiences he had been given would make him a wiser king. He discovered a compassion in his heart that seemed to reach out to everyone. He was beginning to Love. He stayed for a moment by the oak tree and rested within the Light before he got up. He was ready to go now and accept his birthright. So he walked in peace to the village, gathered a few things, and embraced and thanked those who had given and shown him so much. He turned, and vowing to always live the life of a king, he joyfully skipped up the path to his Home.

It is now time for us to acknowledge and accept our spiritual birthright. When we identify with who we truly are, we also accept to Love God more and permit Him totally into our lives. We begin to live from the Center within. Those first steps may be challenging. But we keep rededicating ourselves and recommitting ourselves to living as One with the will of God, and to let his infinite Love and Light stream forth through us and touch all. We will find that as our commitment to our Heavenly Father deepens and expands, we will open to express His Love in total perfection. Our only choice now is to accept to know that we are kings and begin our journey Home.

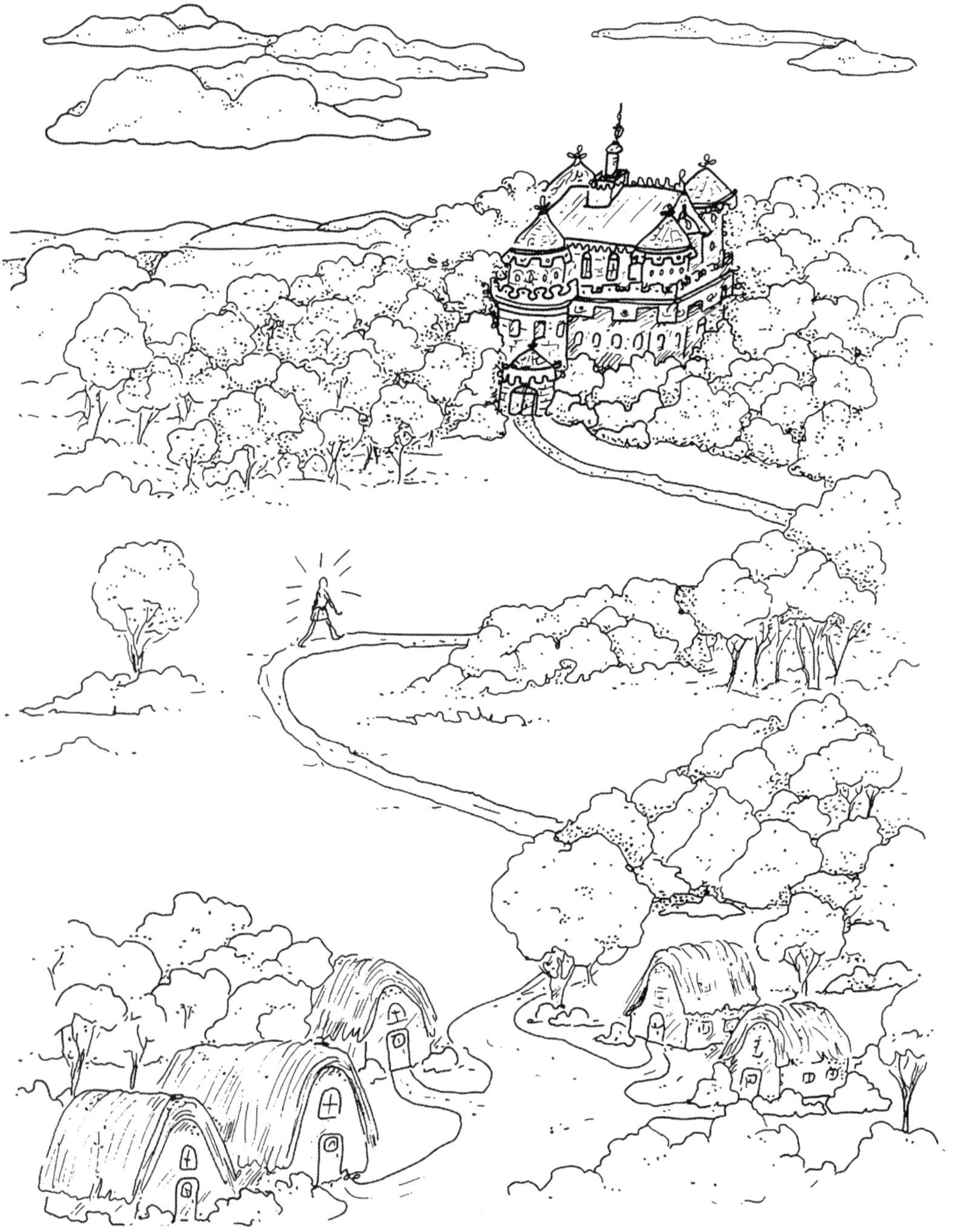

In the Beginning

"I was created in love; therefore nothing can console or liberate me save love alone. The soul is formed of love and must strive to return to love. Therefore it can never find rest nor happiness in other things. It must lose itself in love. By its very nature it must seek God who is love."[6]

Mechthild of Magdeburg

Once a long, long time ago, a Great Being perceived an Idea, and that Idea was of Perfection.

As that Idea took form, Love shown forth, total and complete. Contained within this Love was radiant Joy and Beauty; a Joy that came from knowing the totality of Being, and Beauty from the radiance of that knowing.

This Great Being felt a need to express because all that beauty must be shared. So there needed to be vehicles for the expression of the Love and Joy and Beauty contained in that original Idea.

As this Great Being breathed out, the manifestation of His Perfect Idea began. The vehicles of expression took many forms so that the experience could be complete. Within each form dwelt a spark of that Perfection.

As the Light of Love continued to manifest, a garden appeared. Alive with Light and radiant beauty, it seemed to be beckoning life from the deep recesses of its Being to spring forth. Such Love and Beauty could only be expressed and experienced by sharing at all levels of its knowing.

Some life was quietly expressing that Original Spark as beautiful rocks and pebbles, yet unselfishly sharing all that was theirs to give. Serving in the manner in which they were created was all that was being asked.

Beautiful plants of all sizes, shapes, colors, and forms filled the garden. There was a gentle peace and harmony throughout the garden as each plant, tree and bush, and even blade of grass, moved and breathed as they responded to the Will of their Creator. They too were only there to share and to give back to the earth what was to be given through them. Wonderful fragrances filled the air. Luscious fruits were produced for gifts to passers-by. A oneness of purpose and the Joy of serving permeated the air.

The earth itself rejoiced and gave nourishment so life could continue to be experienced in its fullness. Clear sparkling streams of water sang their songs of love, and also gave, so that all life remained vibrant.

Moving creatures of all kinds were placed in this garden as still another manifestation of that original expression of perfection. In this kingdom, the awareness of the total oneness within that first Thought and Breath sustained the unity and cooperation that was meant to be.

There was giving and sharing according to the needs of each form of life, and the garden grew more beautiful. It was as though throughout the whole garden there was a breathing in and breathing out, a total oneness of expression, and only Light and Love, Peace and Harmony dwelt there. The Will of their creator flowed freely through all that was there, with no resistance. All bowed or swayed back and forth freely as the winds and breezes moved through the garden.

But the Great Being had not yet completed His expression of that original Idea of Perfection. There was yet to be a more complete manifestation. There was yet more to give out so that His total knowing could be shared.

So once again, Love shone forth total and complete. His creation this time was in His very likeness, so that, being like Him, His Idea of Perfection could be known and shared. That Perfect Love was planted deep within His own likeness, the heart of man, and the garden became more beautiful and all life there rejoiced in that awareness of kinship, of Oneness. The Light of Love shown brightly, beckoning all life to live the Love, Harmony, and Peace that was contained in that Perfect Idea.

Man, created in the likeness of that Great Being, was chosen to love, protect, and care for the garden and all the life and Light therein. Deep within his heart was the Love and the knowing that all Life was sacred and connected.

Along with that precious gift, another gift was given -- the gift of free will, the freedom of choice. As a result, man could choose to live in peace and harmony, to allow that Original

Spark to shine forth and to love as the Great Being loved. Or he could choose not to; thus serving only selfish desires.

Seeds planted in the earth needed to be nourished, cultivated, and warmed by the sun to grow strong and bear fruit, and then more seed. Likewise, the Love that lies deep in the heart of man will blossom fully when unselfishness, kindness, tolerance, compassion, and patience nourish it And the Light of the Son, adds His Infinite Touch.

As we walk the earth today, let us remember that beautiful garden where peace and harmony and love reign, where sharing and serving are a way of living. Let us also remember that precious gift of Light and Love that dwells in every heart. And as we walk the earth, remember too that we are that Love made manifest, so that the earth will once more be that Garden of Peace and Harmony, Love and Beauty that it was in the beginning.

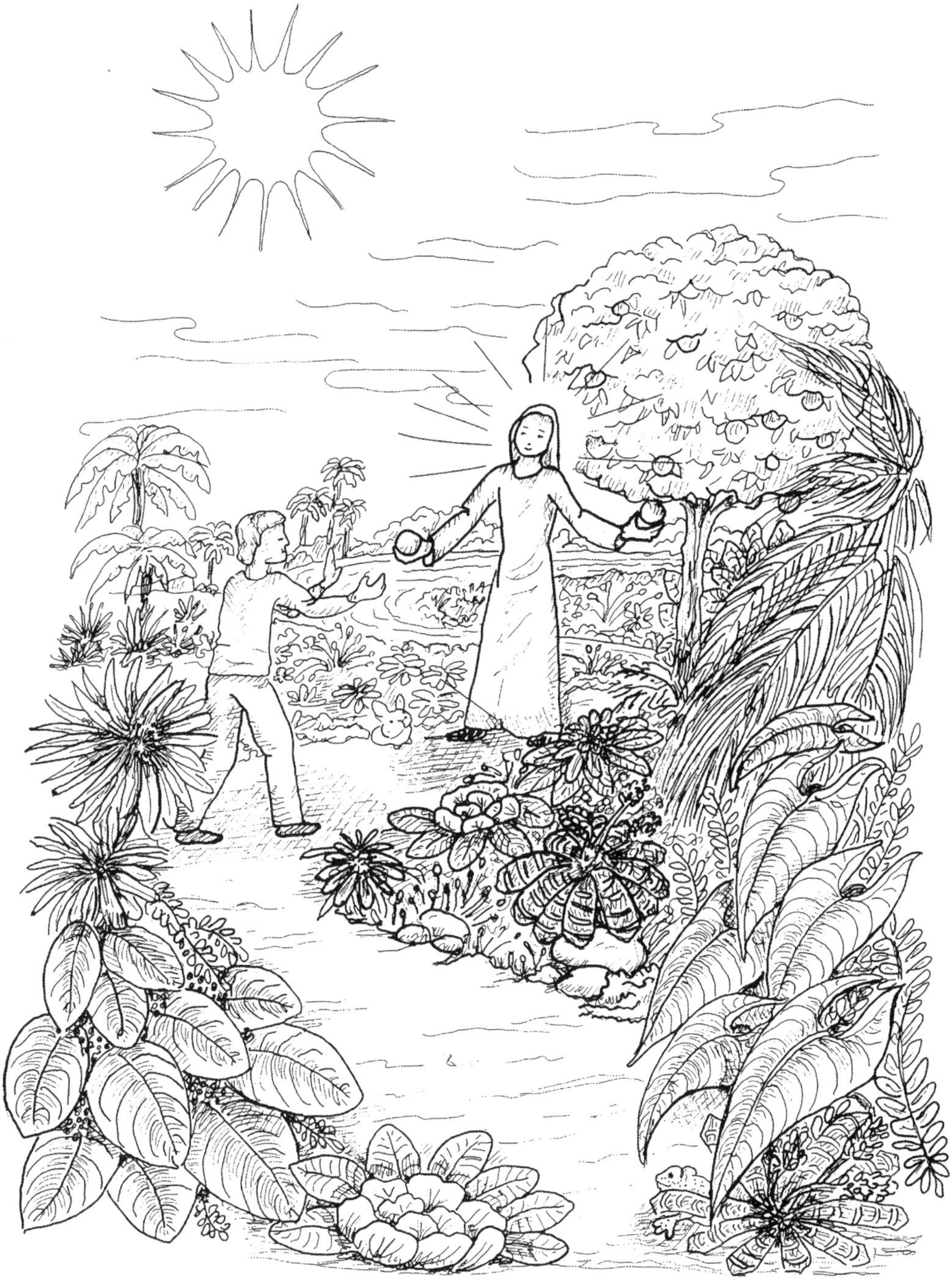

I Am With You Always

"I am ready," Volara exclaimed with a childlike enthusiasm to the two very gentle Beings who were standing in front of her. They looked compassionately deep within her and felt her confidence, yet they also knew of the dangers that awaited her. "You are not fully prepared yet, dear one. Perhaps soon," they replied. With quick determination, she answered, "I must go. I know I am ready. I choose now." The two signaled her to stop and with unison voices sounding as if it came from One, they answered, "You have the freedom to choose your path and you must follow that. Remember always that you are not alone. Within you is all goodness, all purity and that can never be taken away. All that you truly are is Love. You will be challenged and tempted to believe otherwise. But, be still and allow yourself to remember the Light within you, yea, within all creation. You are free, always. Peace be with you."

With those words, Volara departed from the sanctity of the holy chamber which had actually been her classroom for many years. She truly felt that it was time for her to go and try out her "wings" in the "real" world. She had been studying about this place which was really in need of help, for the people seemed to be having a lot of difficulty in understanding how to love and care for each other. They seemed to be confused about the fact that they were to be living as One, following the universal principles of Love which most places Volara had visited before were naturally abiding by. "This can't be that bad," she thought.

Within a short time, she found herself on her way to the new place, the visions of which had consumed all her dream-time as well as her waking hours. Upon her arrival, she was greeted by many friends and felt very welcomed. It was beautiful! The trees were so full with life. Birds were singing songs of radiant joy and everything everywhere had a clarity about it. It all seemed to sparkle brilliantly. She was shown to her new sleeping quarters. "It was all so perfect," she thought.

Soon she became more acquainted with the world outside the complex where she was living. She could feel a slight difference in her heart as she entered beyond the gates of her home. Even though there was no physical fence, there was a subtle change that happened when you stepped over this invisible line. She asked her friends about it and they just kept telling her to be awake. She thought that was a rather odd answer, especially since she slept so little and she felt herself quite alert all the time.

One day she had ventured down a road outside the living complex. She had wanted to explore this pathway ever since she arrived at her new home. There was no real reason for the attraction to this windy dirt road, other than she really felt drawn to find out what was there. Whenever she asked anyone about where the road led she was always met by an uneasy silence and a short reply such as, "You'll find out soon." Once more, she exclaimed, "I am ready," and off she went. As she first began to walk on this road it was thrilling. Something was beginning to happen inside her. She felt so free like she could fly. She felt like everything was wonderful. She certainly couldn't understand why her friends would not want to talk about this road. Soon she began to climb a steep hill and once she had gotten to the top, she stopped and sat down. The view was magnificent. She could see in all directions. Way in the distance she thought she saw people out in the fields. And in the other direction she thought she saw a large type of a building. Suddenly she began to feel very cold and ill. Her throat began to close up. She wanted to shout out for help but she felt herself paralyzed and unable to utter a sound. She could almost feel her body-form changing as the emotion of fear became known to her for the very first time. It was then that she noticed no sound anywhere – no birds, no wind, nothing. She tried to remember her real home. The memory was so fuzzy. Oh, no! She looked up and a darkness, like a thick cloud, was rolling in over the whole countryside. It was coming closer, like a dense mist. It literally engulfed her. She was motionless within it. She felt so strange! She was both attracted and repulsed. She was so confused. For a moment she could remember her home and those two gentle Beings who told her she was free to go but she needed more preparation. She remembered that they said she was never alone. Okay, where were they? Suddenly, she felt two very dark stone-cold eyes belonging to a large male figure, staring at her, penetrating her. They seemed all-powerful. He touched her throat, and the paralyzing fear seemed to vanish. She gazed into his eyes, hypnotized by the pull she felt. Reflecting in that sea of coldness were visions of her in grand states, as princesses of many worlds, rulers over many fellow humans, and holding much influence over the masses. Without warning, she was jolted back to her body by the sound of a bird singing in her ear. She turned her head for a moment to locate the bird and instead she saw two shimmery Beings standing in the distance. In her heart she recognized them, but she just couldn't remember from where or when, for that matter. But as she looked at them, she felt an immense sadness overtake her. Then she caught sight of a little bird flying toward her. It seemed to have come from inside the two

Beings. It was golden in color and flew all around her head. The little bird then began to weave threads of golden Light all around her entire form – inside and out. She felt fully absorbed by those threads of golden Light as they expanded within her and all around to form a soft golden coat. Somehow, it seemed to penetrate and cleanse each one of her cells and hold her safely within an aura of gentle radiant Love.

She gazed longingly at the figures of those two shining Beings of Light and let out a desperate cry as if the sound could have broken the spell of the "cold eyes" she felt she was now under. So painful was that cry, that from Volara's perception the dense cloud became even more ominous and all-encompassing. She squinted her eyes to try to see those two Beings. She thought she saw something gold fluttering about, and for just a moment she was sure she could see the faint outline of two glowing figures.

Consumed by pure horror and despair, she collapsed, folding deep into herself, letting go of all semblance of Life. Staring into the distance, she watched as the little golden bird became traceless. At the same time, deep within the stillness, the angelic voice of the golden bird was singing these words to Volara's aching heart, "Dear child, one day you will remember all that you are is Love, you will know freedom, for you too will soar like a golden bird, responding only to the Voice of God-within. No matter what occurs in the time to come, you can never alter the reality that you are One with the Source of All. You cannot tarnish the Light. Look at your golden robe woven from Light-threads of Love; you are all goodness, all purity. Even at the times when you do not feel my presence or when you want to destroy me, offend me or discredit me, remember dear child, I am with you always, and even after that. Someday, from that point of Love deep within you, you will freely choose to find me. I will be there, for I have never left you. It is so. Peace, dear child, Peace."

It seemed like forever ... but one sunny day this same child of Light found herself staring into the dense fog, feeling the powerful pull of those cold laser-like eyes, beckoning her to come into that world of shadows. Somehow, she stood up filled with a courage that only comes from the Source of Love. She turned her head and looked for the golden bird of Freedom she had been dreaming about from the beginning. She let out a cry which came from deep within time, releasing her from her self-created bondage. Oh, how free she felt. How free! She was in ecstasy as she, for a second, caught a glimpse of herself in the reflection of the Sun. Was it true? The only thing she saw was an incredible golden bird, radiant and all love. "I am with you always," rang forth the Sound of the One, "...

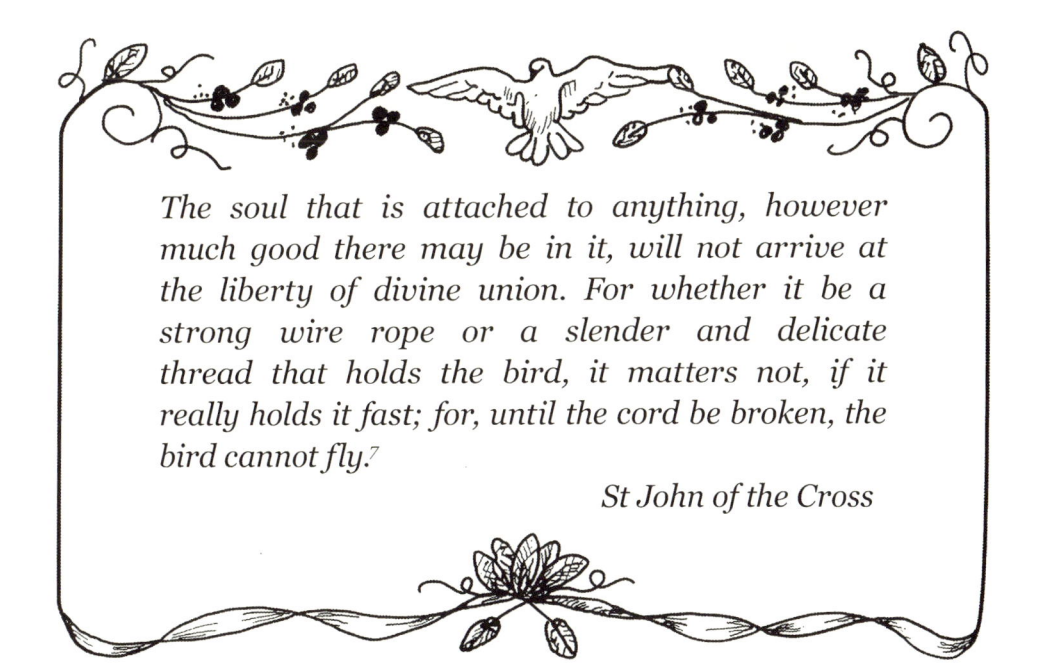

> *The soul that is attached to anything, however much good there may be in it, will not arrive at the liberty of divine union. For whether it be a strong wire rope or a slender and delicate thread that holds the bird, it matters not, if it really holds it fast; for, until the cord be broken, the bird cannot fly.*[7]
>
> St John of the Cross

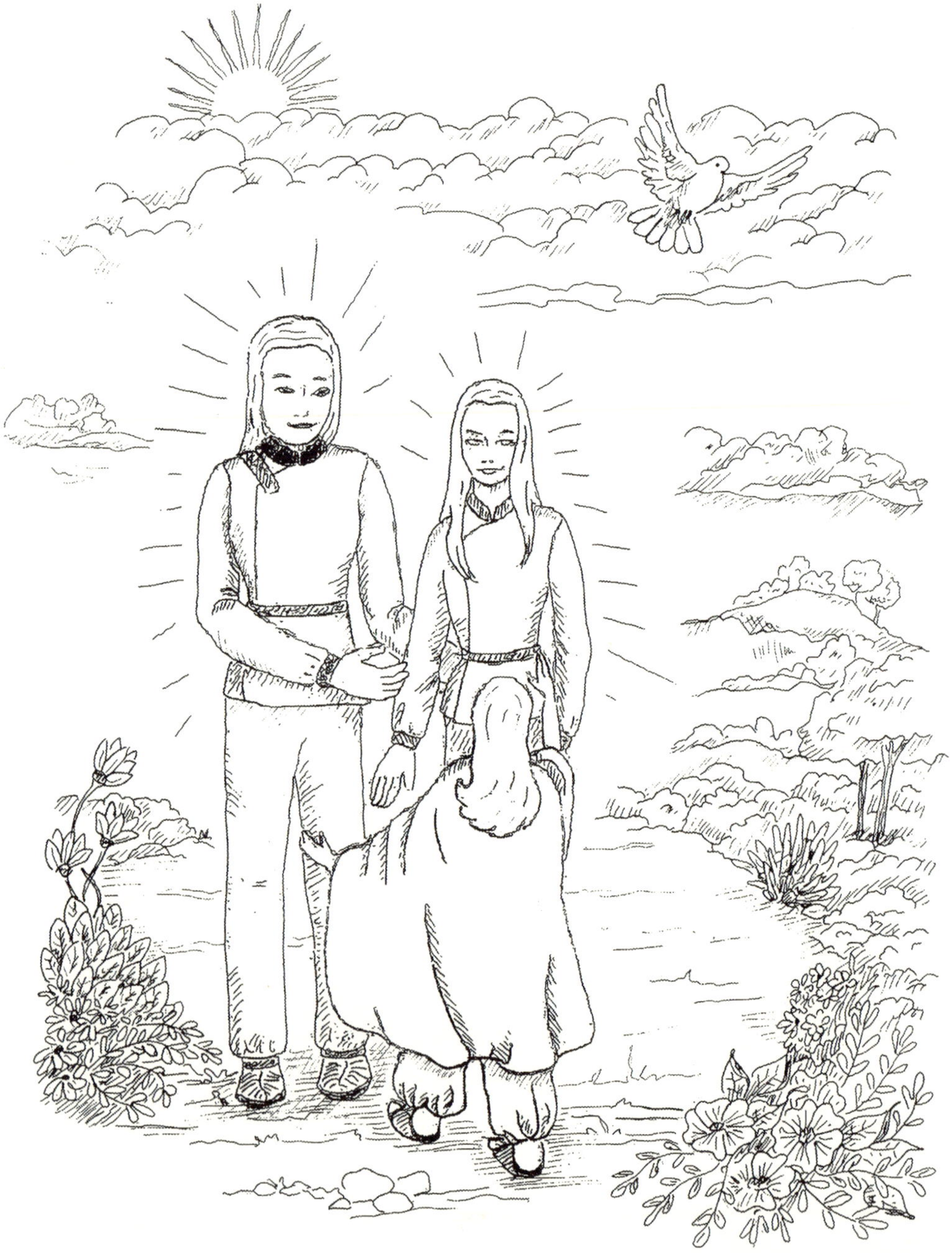

The Silent Visitor

The spaceship glided gently to a halt, hovering just a few yards above the mountain. Its crew launched a small flying craft, occupied by a lone pilot. Then, as silent as the breath, the ship lifted off into space again. No one had seen it come, and no one saw it go. The pilot of the small craft looked from horizon to horizon, closed his eyes for a moment in stillness then opened them again. A mere touch of a button, and the craft wheeled about in the air, as gracefully as a dancer, and then sped off toward the East.

The craft had a transparent dome-shaped cockpit which allowed for full vision in all directions. It flew upon the sea of air, with a capacity of movement that ranged from a stationary hovering, to a slow cruise, to an incredible speed beyond that of the fastest jet aircraft. Maneuverability was the picture of simplicity and ease. With a thought and the touch of a few simple buttons, it could go in any direction at any speed, through any element, and the response was instantaneous. It consumed no fuel and was never depleted in energy. Use, in fact, recharged it. It zotted about from here to there with a freedom unknown to vehicles of the earth; and it was so simple to operate, that even a child could fly it. All around it there shone a soft radiance. Within it, there was an almost imperceptible vibration which was like a quiet hum.

The traveler sped above mountain ranges and beautiful lakes. He watched them as he went by, slowing his craft down occasionally so he could see more closely what passed by beneath him. His heart was touched with their majesty. He felt the call to Freedom singing forth silently through their being.

As He went on, the mountains turned to plains of wheat, corn, and grass. These were soft lands populated with strong people. He felt the courage, determination, and honesty in the people's hearts. Love flowed through him to them, though they were unsuspecting of this blessing. Then came a series of great lakes all touching upon one another's shores, all linked as one, and yet individualized. Here he slowed to a pause – moving so gently as to be barely noticeable. There it was, away just slightly to the south – a Light pulsating with the same frequency to which his own heart beat. He knew its rhythm at once. The craft came about and eased its way down the large hand-like piece of land which seemed to hold all the great lakes in its loving grasp. A moment later, he caught sight of some people in a clearing amidst the wooded hills.

A small group of people, only a handful or so it seemed, was gathered there in a circle, standing tall as the trees, gentle and strong. There was a clarity in their hearts and a joy in their eyes. Their lives vibrated to one purpose. He knew of that purpose. He dropped down slowly for a closer look. His hand touched lightly upon yet another button, and at once the craft came to a halt in mid-air, suspended silently without sound or motion, and then gradually became invisible to the eye. The light of the sun went straight through it, as the atoms of its making became so clear they were suddenly transparent.

Beneath him, the circle began to send forth a pulsation. As it flashed forth through each as one, with the sound of a sacred chant upon their lips, a great Light issued forth which seemed to be at the same time, both rushing forth in a downpouring stream into the center of the group, and also issuing forth from its very heart up to the skies and beyond. The visitor felt the welcome touch of this Light, and a smile shone upon his face. An outpouring of Love rushed through his heart. It merged in oneness with the circle – for their purpose was one and the same, though they knew him not in body, nor did they perceive his craft above them.

He opened his eyes and beheld a spirit of Love manifesting upon the earth, a planet so loved by him – though it was not his home. He was from a sphere so great as to be beyond anything these people could ever imagine. He saw into their very beings. Not all that he saw was Light. Not every shadow was yet transformed. Certain cells within their forms were bound in those shadows. He felt the fear still cringing there, and he remembered the madness it can cause. He saw before him tales from each of their personal lives – each touched with moments of joy, each touched with times of tragedy. He saw the lonely tears cried in the night which no one else ever knew. He saw the sorrowful pain of feeling unworthy when they had known moments in which their weakness overcame them. He saw the joy and the pain of remembering – for their hearts had begun to awaken. He reached into their hearts with his own, wrapped them in his embrace, and said silently within the breath of his Spirit, "My brothers, at last I have found you ... Come, we are going Home."

None heard the voice as it spoke into the ethers – save those whose hearts were already pure. Nevertheless, all those present felt a sudden change – a breath of new life breathed into their spirits. In that instant, their troubles were no more, and their concerns of the world, their weaknesses of the flesh, and their agony of surrender were all forgotten. In that moment, their hearts had opened and were free once more.

A great darkness, like a cloud of foul smoke, lifted from across the earth and was raised high into the air and for a moment seemed to block the Light of the sun. *"Peace," the man spoke, "I give unto you, My Peace I leave with you.*[8]*"* And that cloud burst into countless fragments of Light and was swept away, spiraling upward in a great column of blazing Light.

His craft vanished, and he found himself standing upon the ground in the very center of their circle, in their very midst. The longing in their souls, the joy within their spirit, and the unspeakable holiness of the moment were felt by all the worlds, even though there were only but a handful of people present. Those who had been standing with their eyes closed, bowed their heads in reverence and thankfulness. All were overcome with a Love that knows no bounds, no beginning and no end. Then, one by one, they opened their eyes. Lo and behold, they saw Him still standing amongst them, beautiful beyond comprehension, the incarnation of Love itself. No one could move. All was still. Hearts beat in Joyous rapture. A gentle voice – the only one among the many, who could speak, said "Welcome".

The Holy Man of Light smiled. He opened wide his arms, Love flowed through his heart; and the world was transformed.

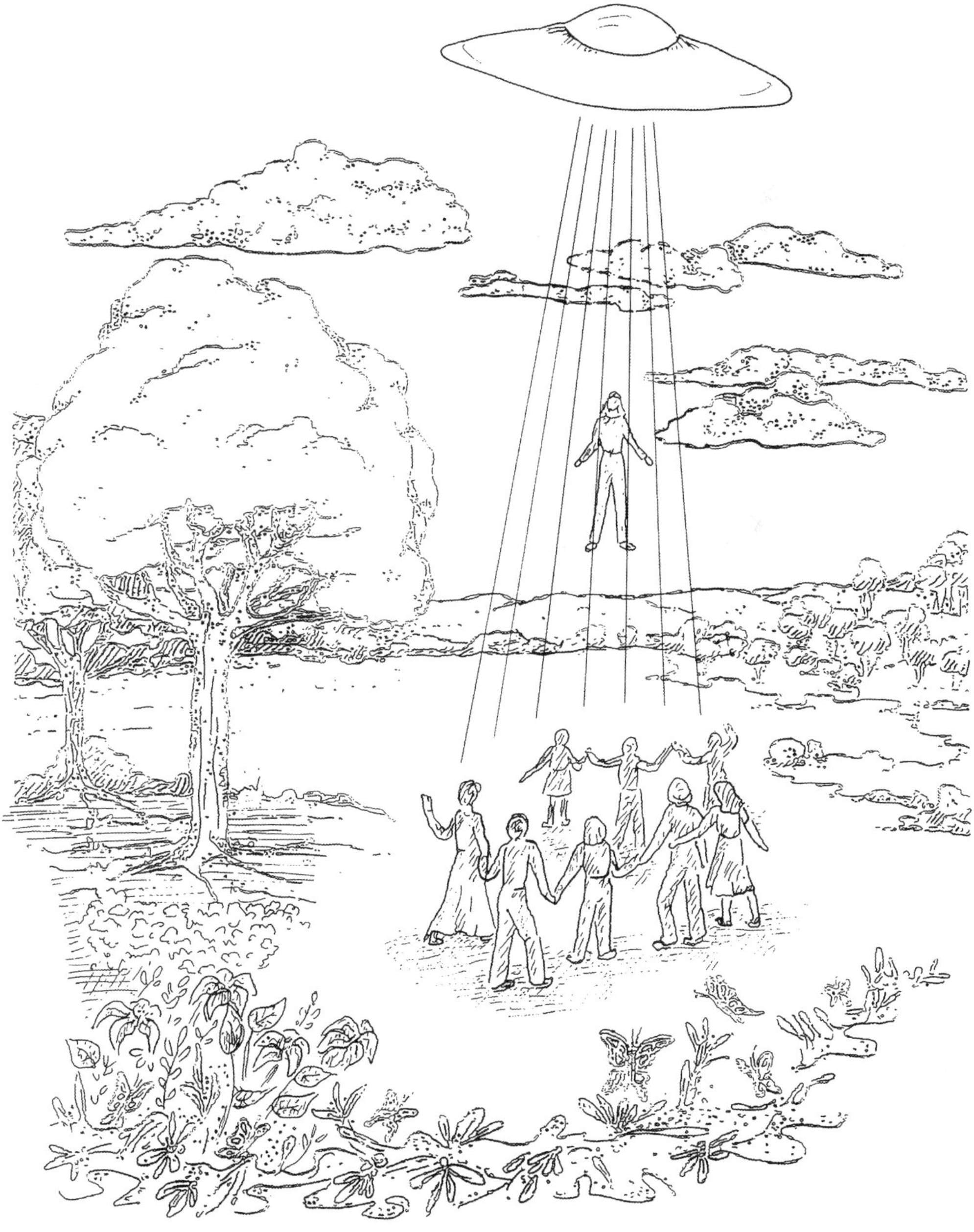

A Dream of Oneness

Now, there comes a Man. Unlike any the world has seen before ... and in His Heart, is an open door through which all the worlds may enter and find the Kingdom of God. No man can say the hour of His coming, but that His coming is near cannot be denied; for His Presence is being felt throughout every dimension; and what is more, it is being felt within the very core of every cell of our Being. And we stand ready and awake before the Light of Love.

His coming will be as it has been foretold, yet also, will it be so far beyond our conceptions as to stagger the imagination. As the energy which He represents -- the pure energy of Love -- is being released in greater degree into the lifestreams of the earth, it leaves no one untouched. His vibration has accelerated the pace of our unfoldment and has startled us into a deeper awakening and a greater realization of what it really means to be the Light Divine. All beings great and small, are feeling a stirring within their very center, from insect to animal to human and beyond. They are feeling something being kindled in their hearts that they have not felt since long, long ages past ... the freedom to be Man – as Man was intended to be ... and this time, man shall be free.

That He might one day truly come, was more than we had dared dream. It was more than we could imagine that this might actually happen in our time. It is perhaps more than we might want to face that He not only has come, but that He walks again among those of the earth as Man, offering us the opportunity to participate in the very work for which He was sent: to allow through His Life, the Kingdom of God to be manifest here on earth. And come He has.

With the dawning of His Presence, incredible changes have also occurred within us ... changes far surpassing anything we have understood before. The way we behave in the world, the way we treat ourselves, the way we feel about things ... our thoughts, our fantasies, our food, our time, our children, our work, our play -- what aspect of your life has He not touched and said: "Awaken! And Be that Pure Light which you truly are. You are free!" What part of us has been able to run from His Presence, or hide from His face? He is everywhere we turn.

Two thousand years ago, many knew that gentle man of Love in body, and heard His words. Two thousand years it has taken for the world to begin to understand His Spirit and to begin to try to live it. Now, that Spirit comes forth through another Man --- the long-awaited Holy One. But do we know His features? Have we learned His name? What do we know of Him in body? ... This time, we must not ask Him to serve us, though He is always serving. Nor are we to love Him more than God, or serve Him as a person. This time, we are to give ourselves totally to God, and seek to be of service in whatever way we are called – be it teaching, or listening, or writing, or emptying garbage cans. This time we must want to serve, not out of fear, and not for reward, or even for our own spiritual progress; but rather, because we love God so much that we want to know and follow only His Divine Will.

The coming of this Man does not make it feel easier on us. It makes us look ourselves squarely in the eye and say: "Who am I really, and what do I want? -- How willing am I to be free? How much do I really love God?" His eyes will look into our innermost depths, and He will know all we have ever been and ever will be. Yet, His eyes will be gentle and smiling, dancing with that soft joy that is ever-flowing forth from the fountain of His heart.

His work will uplift. His touch will transform. The very sound of His voice will comfort the aching heart, like a precious balm. He is kindness itself. Yet, His word will also cut through the illusions of our life like a razor and sever the bonds of our attachments. There will be no more excuses, and no more masks to hide behind. He shall cast the bushel off so that the Light within might shine forth. But, we do not have to shine so brightly if we do not want to. We are free to choose. For, He comes like the silent breeze and enters only where He is welcome. But if we would let His hand rest in Love upon our heart, then we must be prepared for transformation to occur. And if we would have Him enter our home, we must see to it that it is worthy of His entering --- and that all our brothers and sisters who also enter therein are treated in the same manner as we would welcome Him. *"Whatsoever you do unto the least of these, you do also unto me."*

If we think that we can totally manifest the Light within and, at the same time hold back, setting aside dreams, time, and other things for ourselves, we need to ask to know more of what is Real. That Eternal Spirit of Love keeps nothing from God and allows all that is given unto Him by God to flow freely through Him. He is totally free. All the fullness and majesty of the Light and Love that is God flows through Him every moment. Those who are called to serve God are called to serve <u>as</u> God. Their lives become God's and what is more, God's Life becomes theirs. This is the Oneness in which Man was first made and is meant to know forevermore. It is the Oneness that Man was meant to manifest throughout his life and that all creation shall experience. The time has come. And the two shall be One.

Answering the Call Within

How often during the day do you spend time and reflect on what God is all about? What is His Divine Will in your life? How much do you center yourself with His Will and respond to it? You all have felt the Call many times. It sneaks up on you when you're not looking and gently reminds you to raise your vision upwards; to reach higher and to settle only for that which flows in harmony with the Will of God. That Call is from the Heart ... beckoning you to Live the Kingdom of God, NOW; to get on with God's business and to break out of your shell of personality and "ego" and move into operating from the Soul level.

You have the ability to respond (responsibility) to that Call or you would not be continuously hearing it. Sometimes, it seems so difficult to let go, for you do not see the total picture. Apprehension and fear may slide in when you realize you don't know all the details, and especially when you realize you don't know what the results would be if you did let go. But, look a little deeper – the most beautiful thing happens just then. You find you have to trust; trust more than you ever have before, and trust God is there, caring for you, loving you, and asking that you let go so that He may take over and LIVE your life. It seems so simple, doesn't it? Then why do you make it so complicated? Especially after you've experienced that when you open yourself to that Infinite Love of God, let Him in, and answer His Call to live according to the Divine Will, not your "personality" will, your life seems so much more joyous and fulfilling. Then, why the difficulty? To begin with, changes in habit patterns usually don't occur overnight, and you've put a lot of energy into living the way "you" want. So, be patient as you watch yourself radiate and blossom and, as you begin to live your life from the very Center of your Being ... The HEART. You will find the more you respond to the Inner Calls and allow God to be "The Boss", the more opportunities to understand your Glorious Light Within will come your way. It takes courage to make those first steps, to trust, to let go, and to live from the Heart. But, as you might have experienced already, it does get easier. Your life may become more eventful. Tests and challenges will be given to you in order for <u>you</u> to see how serious you are about letting go and honestly living the Kingdom of God.

It's truly an exciting period in your life. You've been waiting for this. Be happy ... the time has arrived to come out of the shadows and into the Light and Live who you are – LIGHT DIVINE.

PEACE   PEACE   PEACE

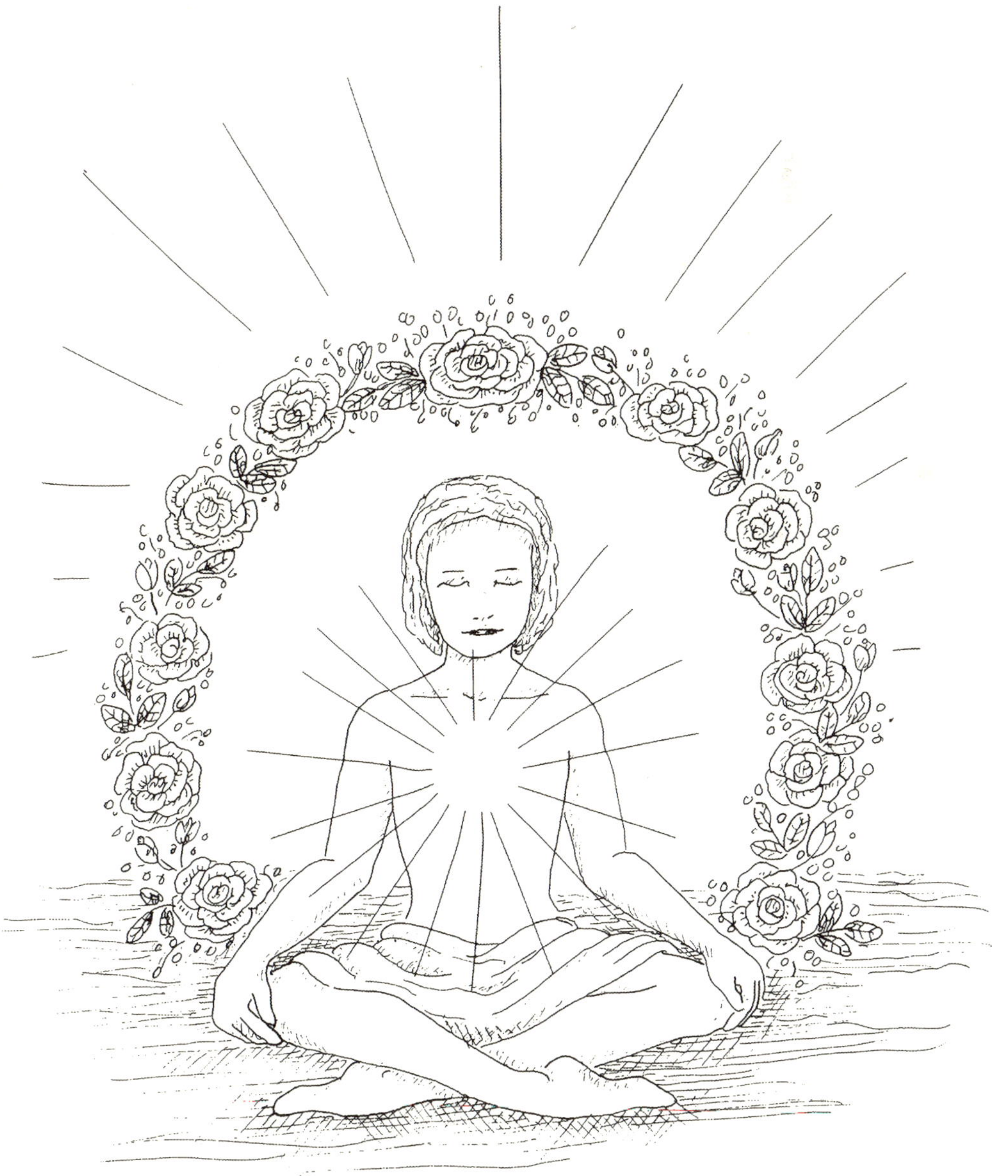

Awakening

Once upon a time, the messengers of the King were sent forth far and wide proclaiming that a sacred gathering was soon to be held. The purpose of the meeting would be to allow all those present to witness a holy event, one unique throughout all the kingdom. There was great anticipation, and joy stirred in every heart who heard, and many were eager to learn the nature of this great event. Finally, all was made ready and everyone, from far and wide, was assembled in the throne room itself. We all were deeply puzzled by the absence of the King's son at such a royal event. Where could he be? And not only were the great and mighty of the King's host assembled here, so also were the meek and the humble servants from throughout all his realms. This must be some occasion indeed, we thought. Perhaps the son will soon appear with the surprise -- the purpose to which we had been called to witness, whatever it was … but he did not appear … Where could he have gone?

The speculations came to an abrupt end as the King arose and addressed the crowd. "My beloved," he said in a voice filled with a Love so deep that tears came to many eyes before we even knew why. "My beloved, I have called you here today that you may share with me in a momentous event, one which brings a flood of joy to my heart." He paused. Everyone's breath was still. Every eye upon him. Nothing moved. The stillness was absolute. The Love that flowed forth from him was overwhelming. Many fell upon their knees, their heads bowed. He continued, "My Son", he said, and as these words came forth from his lips, tears of pride sparkled in his eyes, "has this day gone forth into the Realm of Shadow to bring home again to us all our brothers and sisters who were lost there so long ago". A silent gasp was felt through the crowd as one. The Realm of Shadow! That place to which so many had been sent before and never returned?! The place so far removed from the Light in which we were graced to live that the mere thought of it brought a pain too horrible to behold? A place that had turned from the Will of the King and had embarked upon a course of cruelty too intense to be imagined! He was going there?! After the shock had worn off, a resolution burned within our hearts. Well, if that is how it must be, then let the Legions of the Host be assembled. Let them ride forth with Him in all their might to assail the Shadow and reclaim our own. When do we ride? ...

"Before you rouse yourselves to mount the offensive with Him," said the King, reading our hearts, "I must tell you this: He has already gone ... alone." Alone! "No", screamed an ancient pain from the depths of our being. "No!"

"Be at peace", came the voice of the King -- and the rage of that fear was shattered into millions of sparkling little fragments of Light, like a diamond exploding in the sun, and was no more. A calm fell upon us, and once more we were still.

"Behold", he said gently. There above us, in the atmosphere within the center of our circle, came an image -- living, moving, dimensional. We saw a tiny blue-green planet twirling in space, and a Light issued forth in a pure stream and touched that pretty little world. And her heart stirred. And the purity within her awakened from its slumber -- for beautiful was she upon the day of her making so long ago. And beautiful was she destined to be.

Then came a starlit sky and a small village of humble souls. A woman lay in a manger, giving birth to a son. At first, we wondered what this scene had to do with us; but then, as we gazed upon her face, we saw in her eyes the sleeping majesty of the planet herself, and in her breast, the longing to give birth to a human form. And as we watched, the child issued forth from her womb, and upon his face was the radiance of our King! As the child opened its gentle eyes, there, looking back at us, from a world far removed from our own (and yet now so near), was the face of our Prince, the Son of the King -- in the body of a child! Breathlessness came upon the room, indeed, upon even the kingdom, as we watched.

"This world", spoke the King in a low and resonant tone of affection, "shall, at last, be free". And in that one brief, fleeting moment, every cell throughout every being and form upon that little world opened up and felt the Light.

Years later, some of us now stood in bodies ourselves upon this same world, learning from a man who had once been our Prince. "It is the humble who are chosen, because in their simplicity of heart", He said, "They have no desire other than to serve. Being aware of nothing special or great about themselves, no grand desires of their own enter their thoughts. They are content to be able to serve others. And though they know it not, theirs is the greater Love -- for it surrenders all it has unto its beloved. Even its very life."

Later that week, this teacher of angels and of men – the Son of the King – who would never have had to even set foot upon this world, stood nailed upon a cross at the crest of a hill. As we had watched Him come into the world, now we would watch Him leave (or so we felt). As He breathed what seemed to be His last, we felt the cry of the world, and we understood what it must have been like on that day, so long gone by, when man turned away from his King. The absence was too horrible to bear. How do these beings survive with such pain buried in their hearts, we thought? And how can we go home again to live a life of Peace, knowing that somewhere, even one of our brothers lives in such agony? No, we had to help. We must help. These people must be set free -- and no matter how long or how much it takes, we cannot stop until it is done. They must be set free. Now we understood why we would come again. And so would He. Until one day the heart of the world will open and say, "Yes!"

* * * * * * * * * * *

Then, the sun broke thru the curtains of the window, and this young boy awoke from his dream. "Gee, it seemed so real," he said to himself. "I wonder what it all means?" ... He wasn't sure yet, but he felt that somehow his life would be changing. Then he got up and went about his day ... Meanwhile, a Man of Peace walked upon this same earth and smiled, knowing that another one of His own was beginning to awaken and remember.

The Light of the Sun

It was one of those perfect days. It was so still as the sun began to rise above the horizon. At that very same time, a young boy and girl opened their eyes and ran outside to greet the sun. They were ready for another glorious day of life. As the Light of the sun penetrated deep within them, something familiar began to stir in their hearts. They felt so much love for all. They just knew it was real and could not hold it for themselves. They called out to their friend, the sun, with the simplicity only children have, "Dear Sun, we only want to love so purely that all might know of your Light, of your warmth, of You. Please show us how." Together they heard the exact same words vibrate in their hearts. "Go to the giant tree standing in the meadow only a short distance from here and sit very quietly below him. Embrace his rough bark and ask to know more about Love." The two skipped off to the familiar tree. It was the one whose branches were so beautiful that each time the wind flowed through them; they moved and danced like an angel floating in and out of clouds.

Suddenly, as they were stroking the trunk of this great tree, they felt they were dreaming. They found themselves on a dusty street which led to a few grass huts. As they got closer, they saw a little boy sitting outside one of the huts; He looked so alone, so sad. Now, in dreams, it is known that anything can happen. And so it did. The two young children saw this lonely boy through different eyes. To them, he was only love, very joyous and secure with the knowledge of the love within him, they saw the brilliant sunlight above and wanted so much for him to know of the all-powerful rays of Light. The young girl reached within the pocket of her dress and pulled out a fuzzy kitten. They both ran to the little boy and offered him Life. He accepted the little "ball of fur", the kitty, and looked into its eyes with love, and a surge of electricity went through his entire body. He seemed to stand taller. His eyes cleared. Somehow, he now knew without a doubt he could love, and thus he radiated life. As the two left, they looked back, and for a moment they thought they saw a light where the little boy had been standing. It was just as bright as the sun itself. They knew they had just begun to somehow understand a little more about Love.

Through the years, they had many adventures which brought them to a deeper knowing of the ever-present desire within all beings to love as God loves all His creation, freely and unconditionally. One day they came upon a whole village of people of many ages. They saw written on their faces, a pain of despair, an accepted hopelessness, and a fear of something they knew nothing about. As the two got closer, they felt a cold chill pass through their bodies. They strained to find the sun, but it seemed to be hiding behind layers of dense fog. Even so, they kept on walking straight ahead into the heart of the village.

They stayed with those villagers for a long time until the day came when they knew the sun was to shine for all to see, if just for a moment. They gathered everyone out into the center of the village square and began to speak to them of the original purity and innocence within each and every one of them. They showed them visions of Love that were their true expressions.

The Light of the Sun

Within all of the villagers the cry for freedom, for some real, was awakened. The two recognized the familiar sound of pain and then together gazed into the sun which was just then rising above the horizon.

The voices of the two sounded like the sweetness of angels as they sang forth, "Oh, Divine One, Thy will be done in us and through us. May we all know we are One. May we all know we are Love. May we know You." The two reached deep within their hearts and each brought out a ball of Light and tossed it into the air. The two balls quickly merged, as if they had always been one. It seemed to last forever, and yet all this happened in just an instant. The fog lifted and everything was glowing with a radiant Light. Each villager turned to one another with open eyes and open hearts. They wept tears of joy. All goodness was theirs. They experienced Love. They knew that Love was all there was and all they were. Nothing else existed. They embraced one another and vowed to live this moment forever. And, so they are.

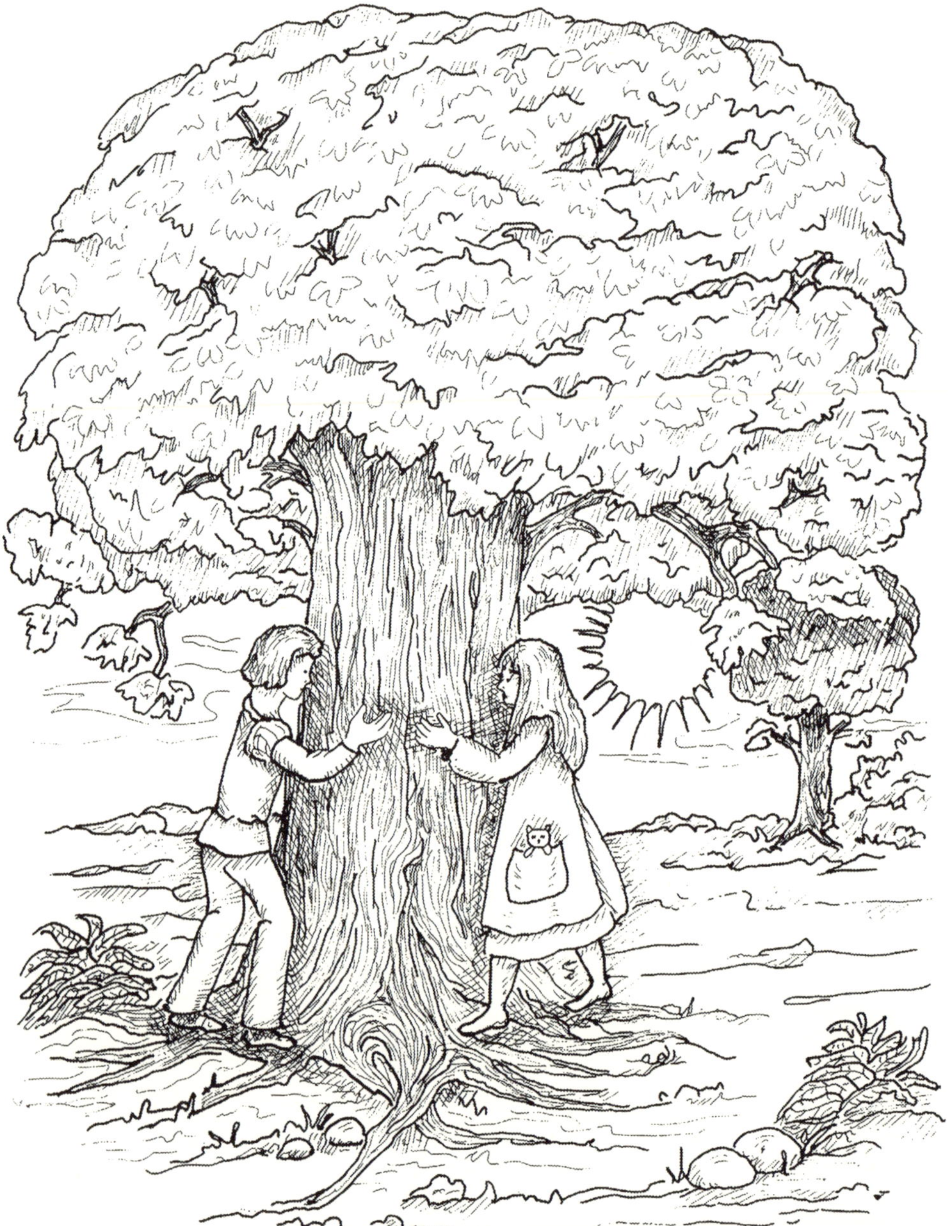

The Year of Awakening

We have passed from one cycle into the next and our hearts are full with anticipation of opening more to the Reality of that Eternal moment which holds All in all. Do we dare let go entirely, to be merged in the ever-present Love of God? Is this state of consciousness for only the few, or is it real for all creation? Is this the year that the vision of who we are as One is graced through all our being and lived in actuality? Do we dare hope that such is our natural inheritance? The answers of course are yes. We begin this year with a renewed determination to open to the everyday gifts which, when unwrapped, we see as opportunities to know God in all. Can we not unlock that door within which may have been shut for so long, to simply allow God to be God in us? This requires the humility to learn, moment by moment, what this means; to discover as a little child, the beauty of God and Love existing everywhere. Humility is not the state of feeling small in the face of knowledge, but rather being at awe with all that is being discovered and understood at the precise moment of experience, holding no expectations, but simply being absorbed in the eternal present; to experientially know God within all. We are on the threshold of such Conscious Awareness. It is inevitable, for that is our true nature: to awaken to who we are as One, dissolved in the One.

How long does it take to come to the understanding that in order to truly know and consciously be one with God, all of our *"ourness", "the ego cage of I and mine,*[9]*"* as the Bhagavad-Gita says, would need to be let go of? Throughout all the sacred writings on this planet, it is said over and over in many different ways: we must lose ourselves to find ourselves. The importance of our separate identity, of all our attachments to how others value us, of our separate achievements in "our" fields of expertise – all of those elements dwell solely within the *"ego cage of I and mine"*. With that intense all-consuming desire of the heart to truly be free and soar on the illumined wings of Reality, to know the All in all, we will burst through that cage and *"pass from death to immortality*[10]*"*. This is the year to awaken, to move out of slumber, to dare to live, to let the hopes and desires for Life emerge, and to live the vision of Divine Love with humility and awe. Gandhi so beautifully put it when he said he was a very ambitious man, for his sole ambition was to reduce himself to zero. So, like Gandhi did during his entire life, may we embrace this time we have been given and may we be filled with such an insatiable desire to know what is Real that we truly lose ourselves, become zero, only to be filled with the Conscious knowing of that which is All.

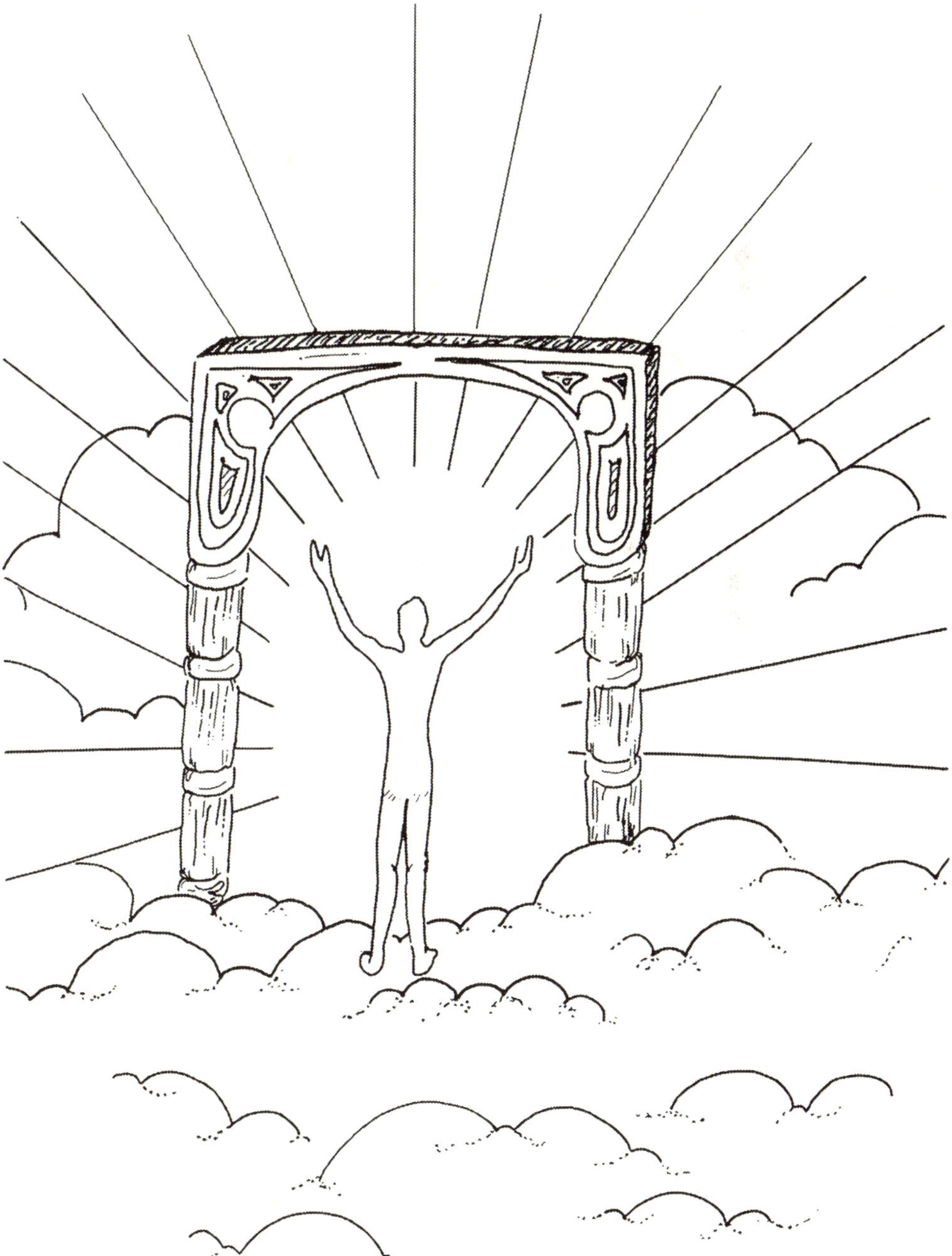

The Blessing of Fullness

There was once a young man traveling down a long, dusty trail. It seemed like it was a never-ending path, filled with loose stones and dotted with giant boulders in very strategic places. He had started on this trail long, long ago, when the world seemed happy and content in itself and when all life forms cooperated with one another. When the "Day of the Shadow" came, as he called it, he forgot much of the simple ways of life and woke with a feeling of deep emptiness inside. Ever since that day, he vowed to fill that abyss with something everlasting, something of substance. So began the first step of his search.

As the sun rose early that morning, Misha, the young man, felt something in the air. He watched the sun as it peeked above the horizon. And, just for a moment, he thought he saw a figure emerge out of the center of that gleaming white ball of Light. He rubbed his eyes. The figure seemed to have disappeared. But it had looked so real! Misha sang a little song, just as he did every morning. He never knew why he sang, he just did. It was a simple song asking the birds in the air, the trees and animals of the earth, and the sun in the sky to be his friends and come walk with him on his search, his journey. Today seemed like a special day. Yes, he felt it. Even his body began trembling when he thought about walking today.

Finally, after a small meal of berries and fruit, he started out. As he walked, he looked straight ahead. The path was quite compelling today. It was as if it was pulling him ahead. Misha stopped abruptly. There – he saw it again – that luminous figure from the sun. He knew he saw it this time. He was not imagining it. And yet as soon as he blinked his eyes, the figure was gone. He decided that he would try to find that figure and talk with it. He found himself running on the path straight ahead, in the direction that he last saw the mysterious figure. All day long he walked and ran, hoping to catch just a glimpse of this Being again. But all was to no avail. He was just ready to sit down in the shade and take a break when he heard a most disturbing sound. It came from behind one of the larger boulders, and it was a most mournful cry. Moving slowly and carefully in the direction of the sound, he encountered a most beautiful fawn with deep brown eyes filled with sadness. Such an innocent creature! It had its leg caught in a trap which was hidden and set close to the boulder. Misha felt a surge of mixed emotions welling up. What for? Why would anyone want to destroy such innocence, such gentleness? He knelt down, stroked the little fawn's head, and then opened the trap to free its leg.

As soon as that was done, he heard singing as if coming from a choir of angels – such was the beauty of the sounds. And then it happened. As he was gazing at the fawn, he noticed it began to change. The fawn was filled with a Light as brilliant as the sun and the little one began to grow and grow until it was the same size as Misha. Slowly, the transformed figure turned around to face Misha. He felt as if he was going to faint, for he recognized that Being as the same one which emerged out of the sun earlier that morning. Misha was both excited and filled with awe, as he had finally met the Illumined One.

Then a wondrous thing happened. It was as if all the days and years of pain and suffering, the thoughts of separation, the loneliness and despair, and the overwhelming sensation of self-doubt came to the surface and overtook him. Misha fought back the tears and the cry which began to well up from the very depths of the abyss he had been trying to fill. "Not now!" Misha thought. "Don't come now! Please stay calm! Don't let go now, just when I'm about to talk with this Being from the Sun." He looked with questioning eyes into the Illumined One's all-knowing eyes and there saw a Love which he dimly recognized. Suddenly, the cry which was so deep within came out. It shook the earth … the boulders rolled and the trees stood alert. It penetrated everything everywhere – such pain and desperation were in that sound. Empty, Misha collapsed to the ground.

The Illumined One stooped down, held Misha close to His heart, and softly spoke these words to Misha's heart: "My dear Child of Light, I have watched you over the years, walked with you and even played with you at times when you needed a friend. You may not have recognized me then, but now you can see I was with you always. I was there on the "Day of the Shadow," urging you to find me, hoping that with each step you made that you would get closer to finding me. Now it is time. It is time to recognize that you are a Being of Light, flowing through the Sun. You do not need to doubt the beauty, Love, and wisdom inside, or doubt your heritage as One from the Sun. God, the Infinite One, awaits your return into full conscious awareness of Him within your very life. Do you not see that this is precisely what will fill up your empty abyss? You are made for loving, to love yourself, and all others as you have loved me. Let this day be a new beginning. Now, look at your emptiness, dear Misha, and behold how it has been filled."

With that, Misha looked at the spot within his body that he had always felt was an endless pit of tears, and what he saw was wondrous. He saw the fawn, the trees, the birds, people he knew, faces he couldn't remember, his family, the past,

AWAKENING – A Journey Within

and he saw himself. Inside each form was a glowing Light, a beautiful glowing Light. The separate lights began slowly to merge together, and there in incredible splendor was one Light, one jewel, like the sun. Somehow it all made sense. He was ready now, ready to know All and not doubt anymore, ready to truly live as a Son of God: happy, loving, and with deep humility. And for the first time in a long time, Misha felt full.

The Little Chalice

Once upon a time, there was a little chalice named Anstead. He was filled to the very top with Living Water that cooled, refreshed, and uplifted the Hearts of those who would partake of its essence. Anstead wanted nothing but to give of this life-giving fluid, that others might quench their thirst and feel that warmth in their Heart. Thinking nothing of himself and his own thirst, he began to offer refreshment to all those who happened along. Many were given help in this way, and encouragement that brought them one step closer to giving of themselves. Some made it to the end of their journey when, perhaps, without his help, they may not have made it. Anstead knew none of this …

One day, as Anstead was sitting and waiting for travelers to come along, he began to think about the Living Water he held. It had never even occurred to him before this, to wonder where it came from. Yet here he was wondering: Where did it come from? How did it get here? How was it that he was always full, never seeming to use up the precious fluid? "Perhaps," he thought, "If it were possible to run out of Living Water, then he might be near the end!" "No," he told himself, "There has always been an abundance of Living Water, and there always will be." "But, what if? …," that little voice in his head said. "What if you could run out? What would happen to you? You would be an empty shell, useless and wasted. No one would like you anymore. The only reason they liked you was for the Living Water that you gave!"

As Anstead was thinking these thoughts, a traveler came by. The traveler had a tremendous thirst. Seeing the chalice and hearing Anstead's happy greeting, he quickly sat down and took Anstead in his hands. The traveler lifted Anstead to his lips to drink, but Anstead began to tremble with fear! He was afraid that the Living Waters might run dry. He didn't want to disappoint the traveler because he knew how great was his thirst. Even so, he was filled with fear.

The traveler began to drink. A look of surprise came upon his countenance. He raised up the chalice and peered within. It seemed to be empty! It was strange, too. It was not sweet as he had expected. It was not nearly as refreshing or uplifting as it had been in the past. There seemed to be a bitter aftertaste, too. He put the cup down, wondering what had happened. What could have brought about such a great change?

Anstead felt numb. He could not feel the presence of the Living Water within. He had never known a time when it was not. It had always been there. Anstead began to cry, dry little tears of such great sadness. Without the Living Water, without being able to give to those in need, there seemed to be no reason for his being. He wanted to curl up in a little ball and hide under a rock somewhere. He didn't want anyone to see him, especially God. He felt such shame.

Time passed. Anstead lived on, feeling lonely and separate. Yet, even as he hid, a still, small voice began to sound within his heart. "Anstead," it called. At first, he did not hear it, but, gradually, it grew louder and louder until he could ignore it no longer. He became still and listened ... It was God calling to him. "Anstead," the voice said, "Do you hear Me now?" "Yes," whispered Anstead, listening intently so the voice would not be lost. "Anstead," it said, "Do you remember the Living Water? It was a gift from Me. It was given to you that you might in turn give. The gift is given only when you give first with no thought of return. Then, the Living Waters flow freely from God's Heart and you are filled." The voice spoke again, "Through selfishness and fear you choked off the flow of that which you would give your very life for. All you must do now is let go; open your heart; and above all else, trust. Trust that God loves you and knows your needs. Through His infinite abundance, all will be cared for." Anstead learned his lesson and once more began to give selflessly, that others might be uplifted; and the Living Waters flowed freely once more …

"But whosoever drinketh of the water that I shall give him shall never thirst; but the water that I shall give him shall be in him a well of water springing up into everlasting life."

John 4:14 (KJV)[11]

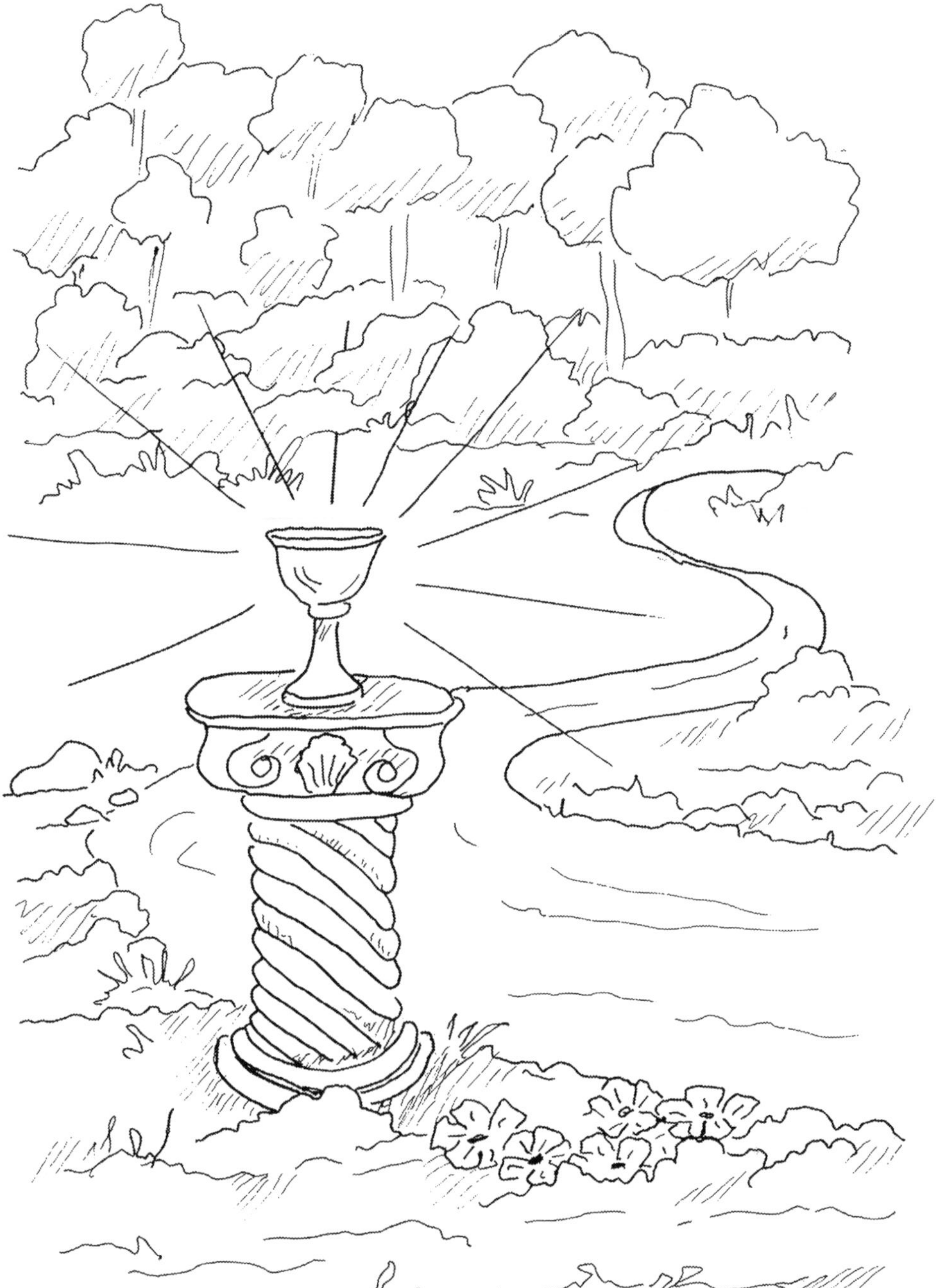

Love is Forever

A long time ago in a small village deep in the desert, there lived a young girl and boy all by themselves. They were isolated from most people, as they had escaped into the desert at a very early age. It happened so long ago they had forgotten why they were even there. One afternoon, a stranger knocked on their door and invited himself inside. With much hesitation, they let him in. He told them stories of the land beyond the desert, and looking deep inside their hearts, he told them of their Father, of whom they had only vague memories. These stories both, frightened and excited them. However, the Love they felt from this stranger was affecting them very deeply and changing their lives. Suddenly, they wanted to know their Father and to love Him. They couldn't sleep at night for they were obsessed with the notion of journeying from their home to the land beyond. They asked the stranger if he would show them the way; if he would lead them to their Father. He smiled and began to walk in the direction of the mountains. Eagerly, they followed.

Days passed. Months passed. Years passed. The children had grown up by now and had undergone many hardships, disappointments. Many times, just as they were ready to give up, the stranger appeared, as if out of nowhere, with a gentle smile and a word of encouragement. Finally, they came to a clearing within this one mountain which they had been climbing for what had seemed like forever. They felt they were to stop, so they did. Inside, they kept hearing these voices, "Is this the time? Do we meet our Father now? What will we say to Him? How do we show Him we Love Him? Oh, we want to Love Him so much! What can we give Him that He doesn't already have? Oh, we feel so heavy? How can we feel Light?

All these questions and more kept running over and over in their minds. Finally, there in the clearing, came an overpowering silence. They looked up and saw a shining Light in the sky. It came closer. They saw people in this Light. They saw an infant. They saw their Father. It looked as if He was holding in his hands an innocent, pure child, a beautiful babe, no more than hours old, and then He offered him to all humanity. Such Love they felt! They could not hold back what they were feeling. They cried and were overjoyed at the same time. It was as if their Father was giving them their own life; as if they were just born. They felt freedom as never before.

Then a hush fell over the clearing. The two looked at each other. They were sure they heard the infant speaking. He said, "Behold, I have come that the world would Know just how much I Love My Father. Now, I must follow My heart and do His Will. Come let us go.[12]" They looked at each other and without hesitation, they went.

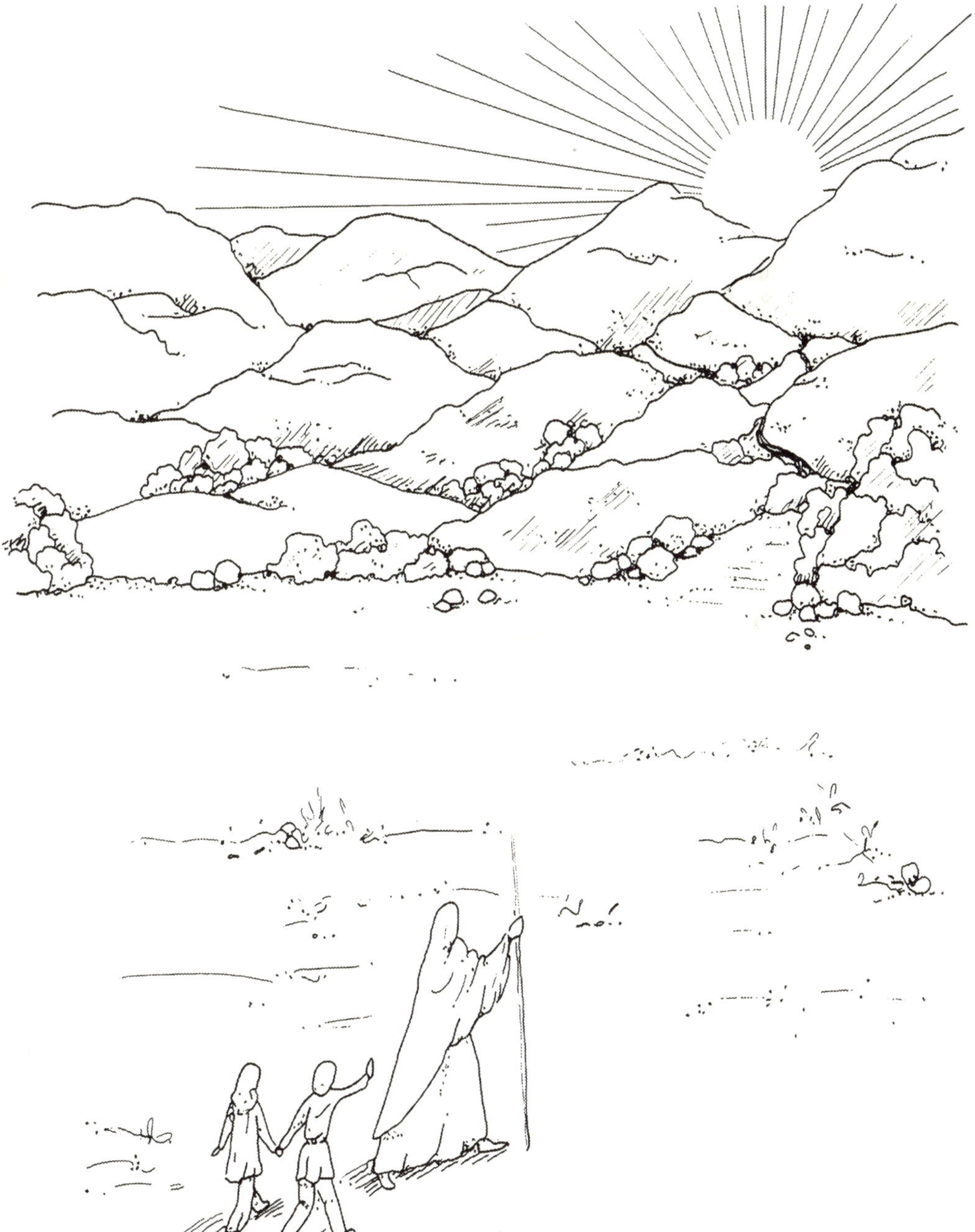

The Manger of the Heart

It was a quiet night in Bethlehem. The air was cold and crisp, and the stars shone brightly overhead. People, gathered from all parts of the country to comply with the Roman census, huddled together in the warmth and safety of the local inns. It was, in many ways, a night like any other. The local folks eagerly exchanged stories and tales with their distant kin as well as strangers, who were all brought back to the city of their ancestors to register, as the new law required. Many of them spoke of family and friends. Most of them had something to say against the Roman occupation. And, some spoke of a Messiah, who would surely come in their hour of greatest need.

Meanwhile, far from the noise of the city, upon the hills, a group of young shepherd boys beheld the glory of an angel and were told the Messiah had come. Much further away, three wise men from ancient lands, caravanned to find the new King, led only by a star and the calling in their hearts. And, at the same time, in a small stable upon a bed of straw, lay a gentle woman about to give birth to her first born son. On a night which was not like any other, and in such a humble place, in such a quiet way – the world was changed forever.

Whether it was recognized then or not, there was a special Light that shone forth upon the earth that night. The simple and pure of heart felt it within their spirit, and it stirred within them the burning desire for a better world – the coming of the Kingdom promised so long ago. They felt a new hope, a new sense of excitement and anticipation – though they knew not why. For the majority of people, the entire event went unnoticed.

And so it often goes that the very Christ Himself comes forth in humble guise, quietly radiating the Love of God to all the world, and by His presence, He changes the lives of all those ready to receive his Light. *"Blessed are the pure of heart, for they shall see God." (Matt.5:8 KJV)*[13]

Whether we understand it or not, there is a special grace given upon the world. In our moments of inner stillness, we can feel the spirit of The Christ moving in all its majesty and power to the very core of the earth herself, speaking straight to the heart of all humanity. There is a call to Peace, to live as brothers and sisters, all children of one God. This call beckons us to give His Love to everyone we meet through service, humility, and truth. It is as if the Christ Himself came forth to each one of us, looked us in the eyes and He laid his Hand upon our hearts and said: "Go forth unto all the world and Be my Light. Speak my Word, carry forth my healing, bring forth my Peace. I am asking you to go in my behalf, and live a life that is pure and holy, that God may be glorified"

Such a call has seldom gone forth with the energy and vibrancy that is now present. If we feel it, if we know the time has come, and if something within us leaps with Joy at the thought that such a Life really is possible, then know that we are among those who have seen His star rising in the Heavens, and are following it to its very Source: a simple manger within our heart where the Son of God is born.

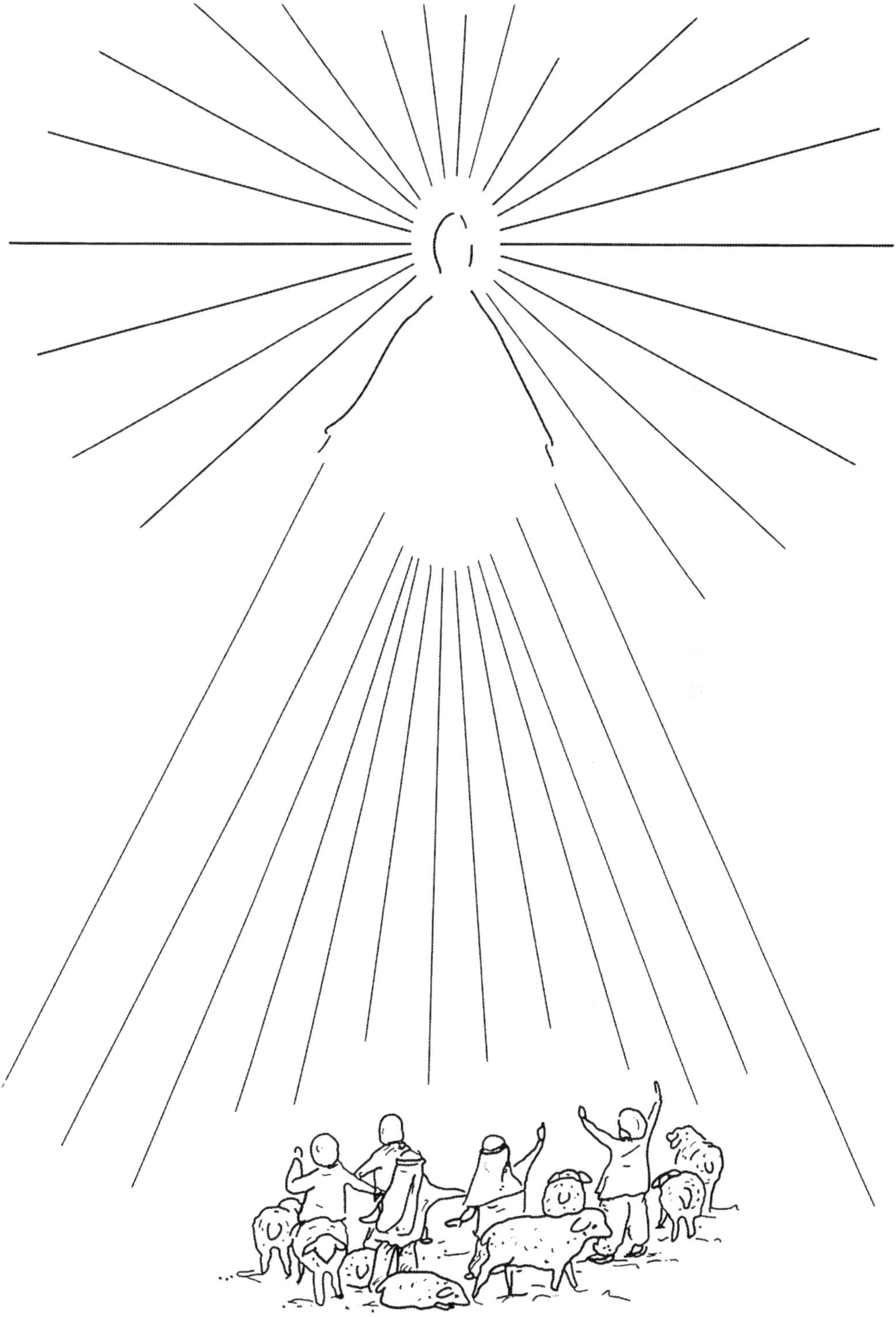

Time for Change

There is something wondrous about that sacred and mysterious time of the year when we celebrate the birth of the Son in such an all-encompassing fashion, that even the most guarded heart has a chance to be touched by the hand of God. The autumn bursts forth filled with fiery leaves echoing their passion for life. Then it gently folds into itself as we await the first glorious snowfall which graces us all with its purity and goodness. As we observe this natural process of the changing of the seasons, we must certainly wonder about just what allows some trees to shed their leaves so quickly and others to persevere throughout the severest of wind storms and still manage to keep some of their withered-up leaves clinging with such determination to their outstretched limbs.

It is truly a fact that the trees are still very much alive with life, even if all appearances are ones of death. But what about that one leaf that does not let go, that resounds with an emphatic, "No, not now! I am not ready yet to just drop into the unknown and die." What finally releases that leaf from such bondage? What happens when it suddenly finds itself parting from the world that has been so familiar to it for such a long time?

Is that leaf not like that part of ourselves that seems to cling to us and not let go? Is it not like the old way of thinking and perceiving the world? We discover those dried up leaves are just like erroneous thought-forms which need to be transformed, to be released so that the fullness of Life can express itself. Sometimes we need many persistent wind storms to loosen the bonds to those dried up leaves. In wanting to know and live only what is real, not our self-created worlds, the storms will be brought to us, in our measure as we are ready, and just at the right time. We can only welcome this process of change and renewal, for soon the new leaves will begin to bud and blossom forth. And one day we will stand back with awe and behold the tree which radiates only the pure manifestation of God, each leaf knowing it is One with the whole. And so it is with us. There will be a day when we shall know and Live only the Will of God. This shall be a time when all our thoughts and actions spring forth from deep within Our Divine Nature, crying out a declaration of Love for God. All expression is then lived only to glorify God. Is this just a dream or is it our destiny? We believe this is a natural unfoldment. Why? Simply because it is our nature as divine beings to constantly manifest greater expressions of God. During this sacred season of Love, let us remain ready to allow the birth of the Son to occur within our hearts – not so that we might become more spiritual, or improve our character, but simply because we love God so much that all we ask for is to open enough for Him to fulfill His Divine Will within us, or as Meister Eckhart says to let God be God in us.[14] This is a glorious season. Live it as who you are: a divine being whose nature is to glorify God. May Peace be with you forevermore.

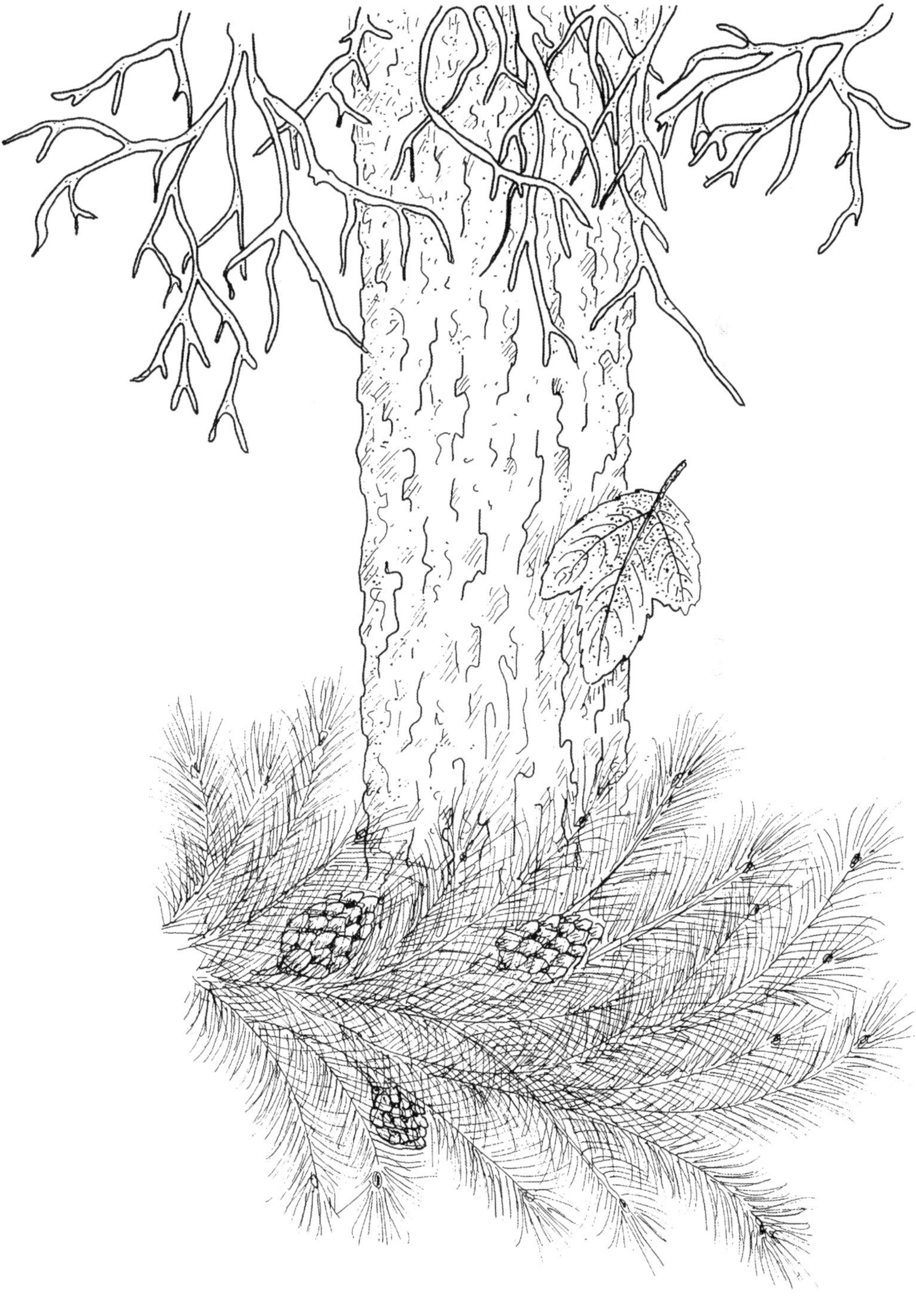

Ablaze With Love

I know the path. It is straight and narrow. It is like the edge of a sword. I rejoice to walk on it. I weep when I slip. God's word is: 'He who strives never perishes. Though, therefore, from my weakness I fail a thousand times, I shall not lose faith.[15]

Mahatma Gandhi

What does it take to set our hearts on fire, to touch that spot deep within our very being which is calling to come alive, to be set free? Quite often it is so easy to witness the fullness of life around the trees with their fragrant blossoms, the flowers with their vibrant colors, and the birds with their constant songs of love. All of these are indications of the presence of God, of His life dwelling within them. What happens when we take for granted His eternal presence or numb ourselves to His beauty, the very existence of life, of God-essence within the form? Could it be then, possible for us to search for and hope to find that same essence within ourselves? The same Divine element which takes our breath away or brings us to tears when we observe the passionate display of life throughout nature is that very same element of Life-essence found within us, within our brothers and sisters and within all creation. Our false pride as

Kabir stated in his poem, must be totally surrendered if we truly wish to seek and find God within. If we don't, we will inevitably be carried away into worlds of our own creation which will only bring us to beautiful pictures of illusions of life but will leave us empty and dry in the end.

It is the prayer of our heart that somehow, someday, we would allow ourselves to forget all about "us", to throw open our arms and embrace within us total life, and to let that life permeate each cell of our body, our mind, and our heart, thus washing away all that is not real. For that moment, as we let go of ourselves, we would be so utterly filled with the knowing of God, of life/love itself, that to return to the world of shadows would no longer hold its appeal.

Then why is it so hard to let go, when all we wish for is to know life, to know God Himself? Whatever reason we may have, we must not let that stop us. We must courageously start, one step at a time, not focusing on the difficulty, but rather on the One whose life is within us, within all creation. That is what is real! That is what allows us to break out of the self-inflicted bonds of slavery into total Freedom. We <u>can</u> let go and be so absorbed in the presence of God that we find ourselves amongst those million suns that are ablaze with Light. Lo, we find we are one of those suns, and finally our heart is passionately alive. It is truly on fire with the flow of Love.

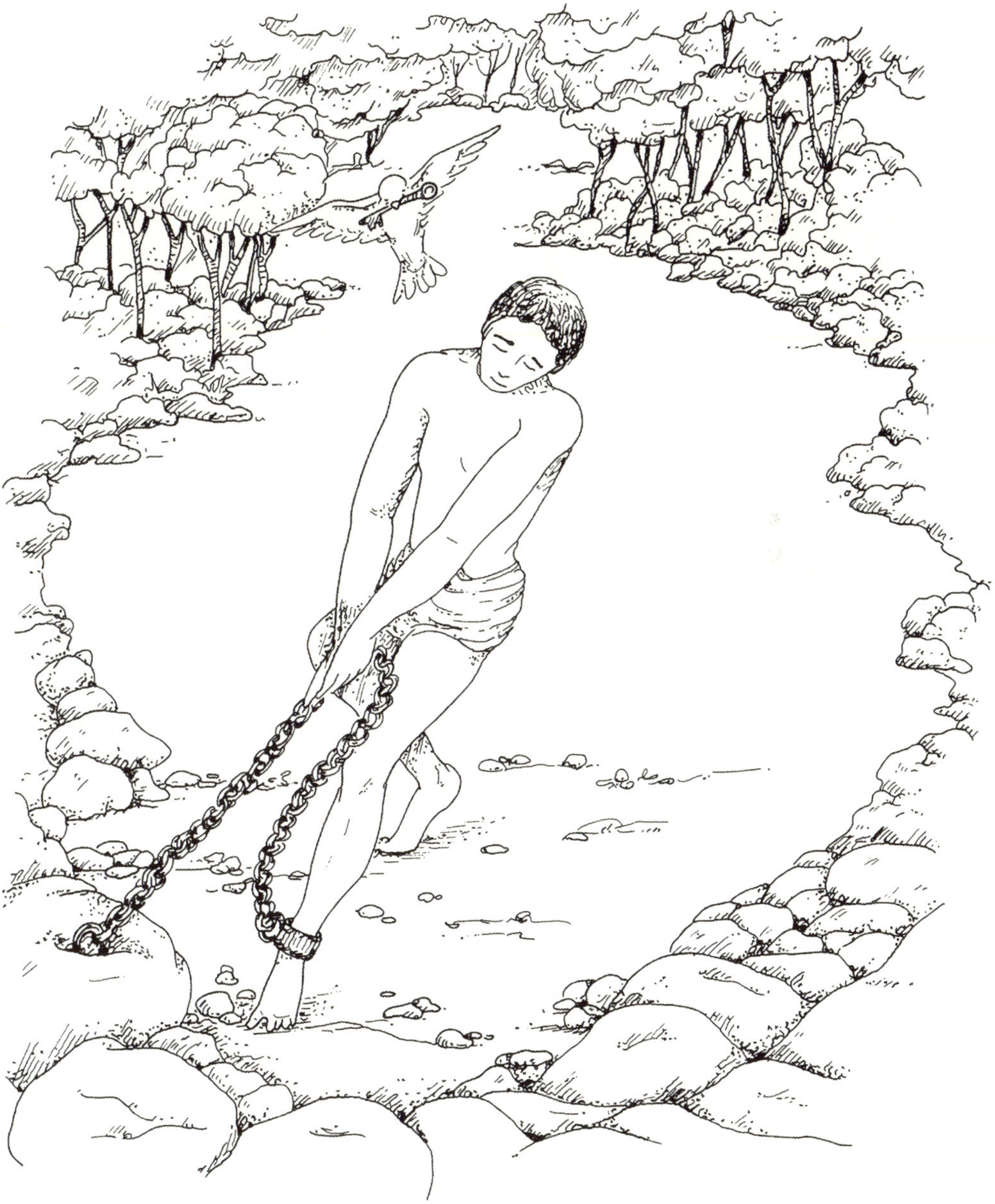

Prayer of Teresa of Avila

I gave all my heart to the Lord of Love,
And my life is so completely transformed
That my Beloved One has become mine
And without a doubt I am his at last.

When that tender hunter from paradise
Released his piercing arrow at me,
My wounded soul fell in his loving arms,
And my life is so completely transformed
That my Beloved One has become mine
And without a doubt I am his at last.

He pierced my heart with his arrow of love
And made me one with the Lord who made me.
This is the only love I have to prove.
And my life is so completely transformed
that my Beloved One has become mine
and without a doubt I am his at last.[16]

Teresa of Avila

The Treasure of the Heart

Once upon a time long gone by, there was a land of beauty – a land of fresh, clear-flowing rivers, abundant foliage, green and tall and graceful; of gentle breezes and warm nights. It was there that fruits, nuts, grains, and vegetables of every imaginable sort grew, each one more delicious than the next; each one filled with a vibrancy and joy one could actually feel. These foods of the land were offered freely to the Kingdom of Man, who shared them together in peace. Everywhere the eye could see, there was balance, and life was in harmony with Life.

From just such a world as this, a man came forth, leaving behind all that was so dear to him. To a distant land he journeyed, alone and without companions. At last, he came to his destination, a small village, filled with the hustle and bustle and activities of humanity. Their attention was so focused upon themselves that most of their time and energy was spent struggling. They fought against their environment in the belief that they needed to control it to be safe. They fought against one another in the belief that there was not enough for everyone, and that only the strongest and cleverest could survive. They battled against pain, fearing to look beneath it and discover exactly what the pain was helping them to discover in themselves. They fought against death, believing it to be the end of all that they had worked so hard for throughout their lives. And they struggled to find beliefs that would make God serve their desires and keep away from them that which they feared. Even when they slept, they were not at peace – for they did not trust in life.

As this gentle man from the land of Love looked deeply into their eyes, he beheld there the same Light of God that he knew in each of the people and creatures in his world. So he spoke to these people in the human village, to help them understand. Some were too busy and asked him to come back some other time. Some were angry with him for showing them so many beautiful possibilities, which they felt they would never be able to attain, and they resented seeing the wretchedness of their own condition in the light of what could be. Some of them feared him, for they felt that he could see into their very soul, and discover there all the selfish and shameful deeds and thoughts they had ever had or done. And that if he saw those thoughts, surely all the world would somehow know them, too. And they wanted to keep these things hidden, especially from themselves. But some of them listened. And some of them spoke with him and asked to understand the land of Love. They wondered if they could ever get there? Yet no matter how they responded to him, his love for all of them continued, and his prayers were for every one of them.

For many years he taught them of the beauty of their own land and how it too, could be – was meant to be – a land of living Love. Something within them, as well as in the very land itself, began to change. There was an opening to Love.

Before his time came to leave them and return again to his homeland, he taught them the secret key to unlock the treasure hidden within all lands, all peoples, all creatures, all creation: that beyond all the activities of their life, all that really mattered was Love. And that when they would finally be willing to open their hearts to Love, their land would be transformed by its touch. The beauty and joy that would thus burst forth would be beyond even their imagining.

"God created all things out of His Love," he said, "and therefore, all things respond to Love."

"But what about the people who don't believe," they asked him, "what about all the cruelty in our world? What are we to do? ..."

"Love them," he replied, "in the way that I have loved you – and trust in God, for all things are within His care, from the very least unto the very greatest."

"Remember," he told them, "that the temple of Our Father is the living altar of your heart. Herein dwells His Presence. Herein shall you come to know Him. And to know Him is to know Love. Then shall your eyes be opened, and with wonder, you will gaze anew at the world about you, and suddenly find displayed there all the treasures of His Kingdom. For my Father and your Father are One, and we are all one within His Heart..."

With this, he took leave of them, once again returning to the land of his birth, where there was great rejoicing upon his return. Yet their joy was not due to his return – for they had never felt apart from him – but rather, their joy was from beholding the Light that was beginning to radiate from that land that had been so distant and so dark before his visit.

"Will they remember?" someone asked him.

"They can remember" he answered softly, "... they can.

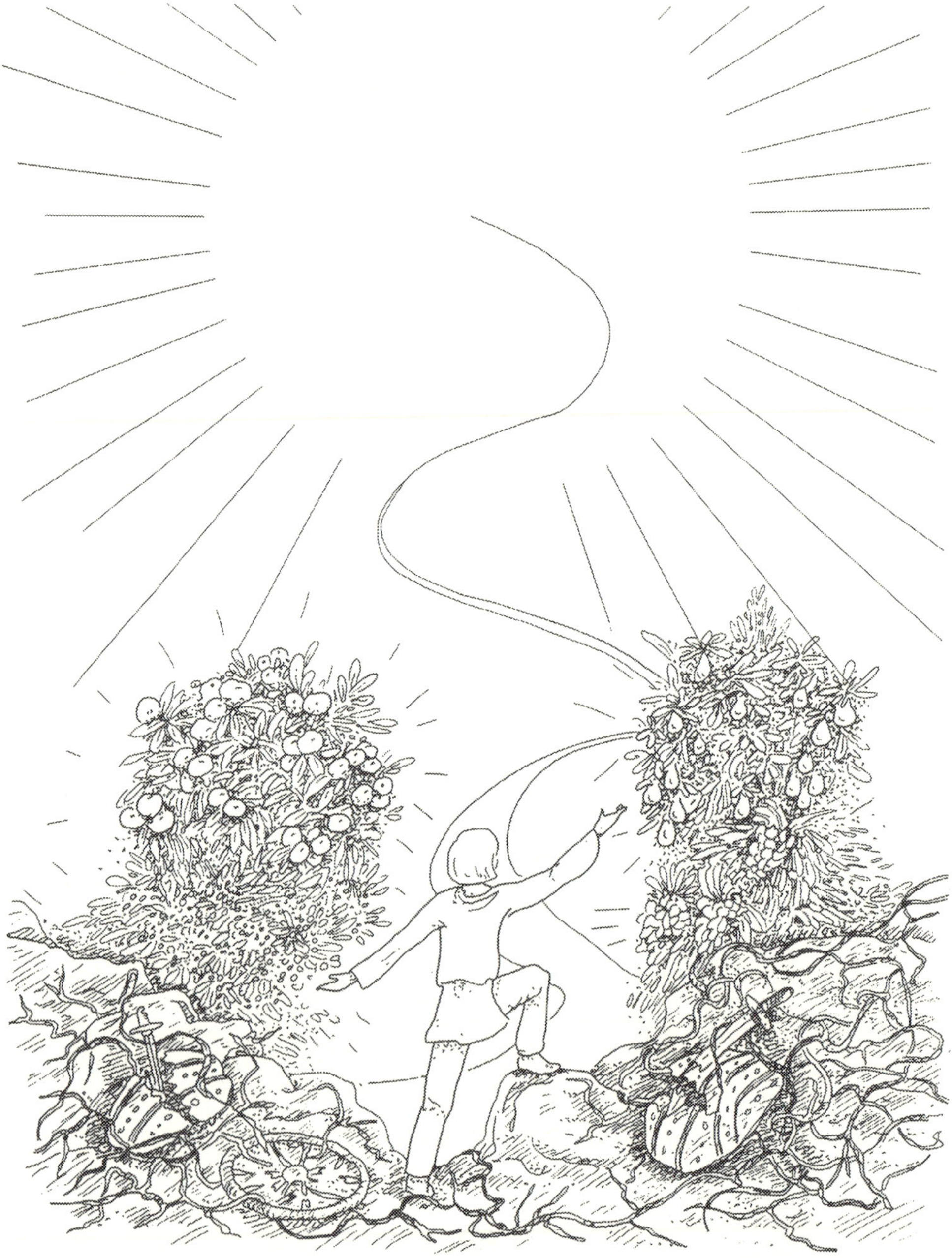

This is the Day

"This is the day! This is the day!" Noltron awoke to those words as he leapt out of bed. Who was saying that? Where were they? He looked out the open window and saw a colorful butterfly staring at him. It was a most unusual butterfly! Vibrant purples, greens, and oranges melted into one another as if the colors were fluid and alive. Suddenly, with the most melodic tone, it began to speak. "Oh, you are awake. This is the day!" Noltron, though he was a bit shocked, managed to squeak out a few words in response to this most surprising occurrence. "What day?" he asked. He then climbed out the window onto the soft ground and settled down to listen to the most fascinating tale. The butterfly began her story.

She had been born with no sight. She was blind and did not know there was anything unusual about that condition. She felt she could see the world around her perfectly. She lived each moment fully. She could hear the world and sense it with her heart. She lived many years like this, being so grateful for the sight within her Being, for it vibrated with the fullness of Life. She embraced each day as a gift to learn more about Life and the Giver of this gift. She never doubted she could see, although many around her told her quite often that she could not see so much as a shadow. Furthermore, many informed her it was never going to be possible for her to gain any sight for she was indeed totally blind. These comments only ignited the gentle flame of Love within her as she knew, without a shadow of a doubt, that she could truly see. To most observers, she appeared to not function like a sighted-butterfly. But that did not stop her. She was so in love with all that she felt in her heart. It was like being in love with Love itself. She saw herself gracefully dancing with the flowers and flittering around the other butterflies. "You can see. It is possible, even if others do not believe. Just follow your dream. It will take you to where you want to go and to find what you seek within your heart. You will see and know what is real." She kept hearing those words echo inside. Then one brisk morning she heard, "This is the day! This is the day! Go and tell others who have ears to hear." She had been flying all morning and Noltron was the first who heard her words. She invited him to come with her as this was the day!

Together they traveled down a dirt path which led into the foothills of the great mountains nearby where they both lived. They were spellbound as they felt they had just walked into another world. They saw an old man on the horizon walking towards them. The butterfly was sure this was someone they knew. She felt it in her heart. He approached them, looked at them with eyes that held within them all of creation. "I know him. He is the Giver of all gifts. He is all," the butterfly explained. "This is the day," the old man replied. The whole mountain began to vibrate. They all felt it. Then, as if from nowhere and everywhere, the mountain and everywhere around it lit up. From the very center of the Light came forth a Sound. They listened with full attention. "I tell you most solemnly, dear children," the voice said, "I have come to show the world how much I love my Father.[17]" There were sounds of angelic voices, birds, trees, and all of creation humming in unison. The little butterfly was beside herself with Love. She felt like she was about ready to burst, yet deep inside such a peaceful joy was stirring. She had only dreamt about Life being so full. Both Noltron and the butterfly discovered, at the very same time, that the old man who was there a moment ago was no longer there. They looked up above. Much to the butterfly's amazement, it was she who spotted it first. She could actually see a form. The old man had changed. It seemed he was All. Then, just for a second, she saw a large shimmery object hovering over the clearing, a little ways down the mountainside. The voice was resounding from deep within the ship. "I have come to show the world just how much I love my Father[18]. So be it. Remember we are One. Open your heart and let go of fear. Just love God with all your heart, with all your mind, and with all your Soul. You can! You can! That is who you are. This is the day!"

The little butterfly, who was now fully aware she had been given the gift of physical sight, was so filled with Love that as she looked at Noltron, all she saw was a Radiant Light. She realized that was all she saw everywhere. Then very silently, with a deep hum, the shimmery sphere began to move. She glanced up and saw a young woman and man holding up a tiny little baby for all the world to see. The butterfly flew closer to see the child. The child opened his eyes. It was the old man. He smiled. "Yes, this is the day.

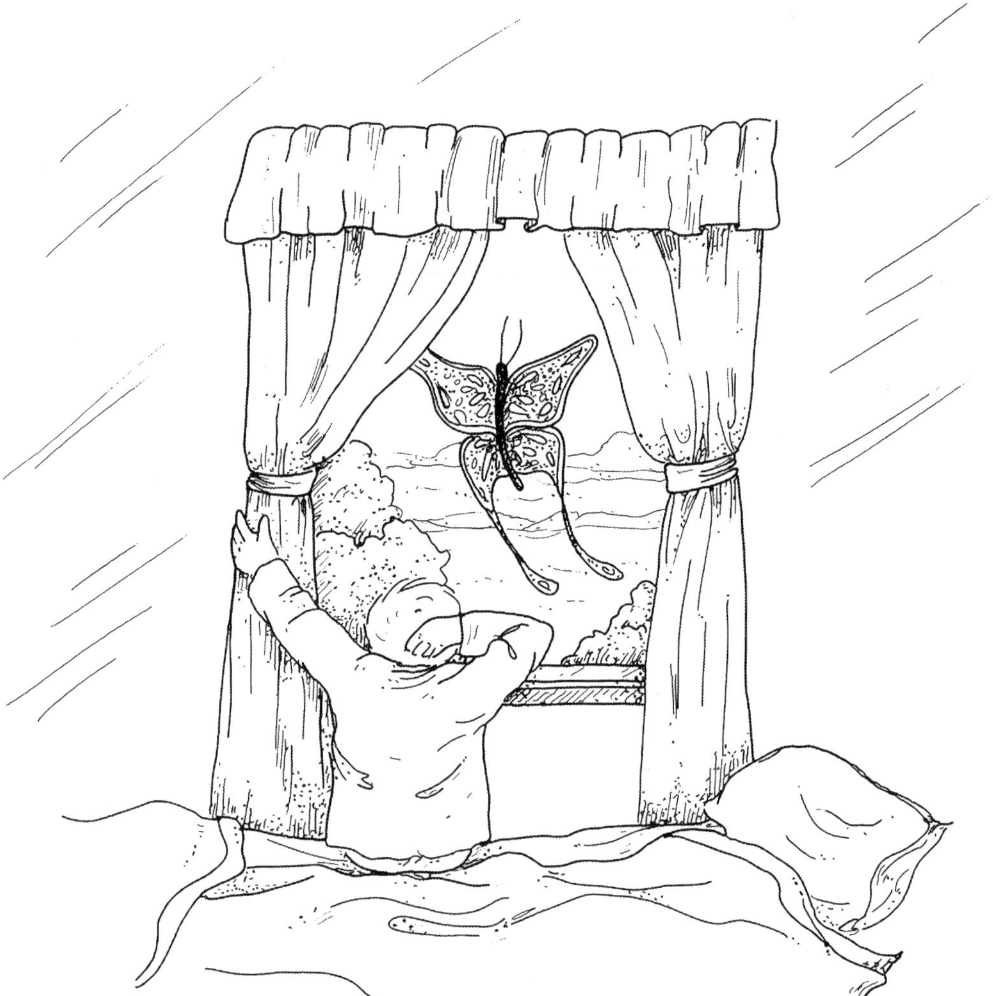

I Am With You

Standing high above a snow-clad mountain top, shining like the sun and radiating as brightly, there came forth the Sound of Love in an even, rhythmic pulsation. The earth herself quieted down, stood alert, and received the gift of Love. The trees bowed; the rivers danced among themselves; little creatures wept tears of joy, and the wind was absolutely still. Slowly, the billowy, rolling clouds unwrapped themselves to reveal deep within a gentle Being of Love. So beautiful was the Light that, for a moment, all breathing stopped everywhere, and the vibration of Love seemed to penetrate every atom of life.

Within the safety of several evergreens, were two little children who had been brought there to sing the Song of Eternal Joy with all creation. Their eyes shone brightly as this gentle Being extended part of Himself to caress them with a familiar touch. Their little bodies shook as the whole forest, the mountain, and the skies everywhere began to be filled with the Sound of His Voice. The two little ones were so much part of those words, they found themselves spinning upwards, tumbling round and round, arms outstretched, eyes aglow with Light until they could go no farther. They were absolutely sure they were the very words themselves.

"My dear children, I am with you. My feet walk this planet now to show you how much I love my Father.[19] It is time you are to be with me, to accept your innocence, your greatness in Light. I carry you within my heart always, listening to your cries of pain and your encompassing call to be free. Lay down your desires for self and soar with me into the original and only desire to be One – the desire to be so filled with the Love for our Heavenly Father that finally, yes, finally, you awake, and you have lost yourself. That is my prayer for you. So be it."

The children and all life forms who heard these words knew this was just the beginning. They would meet this Being of Love again and know these words as if they were their very own … until the end of time and even after that.

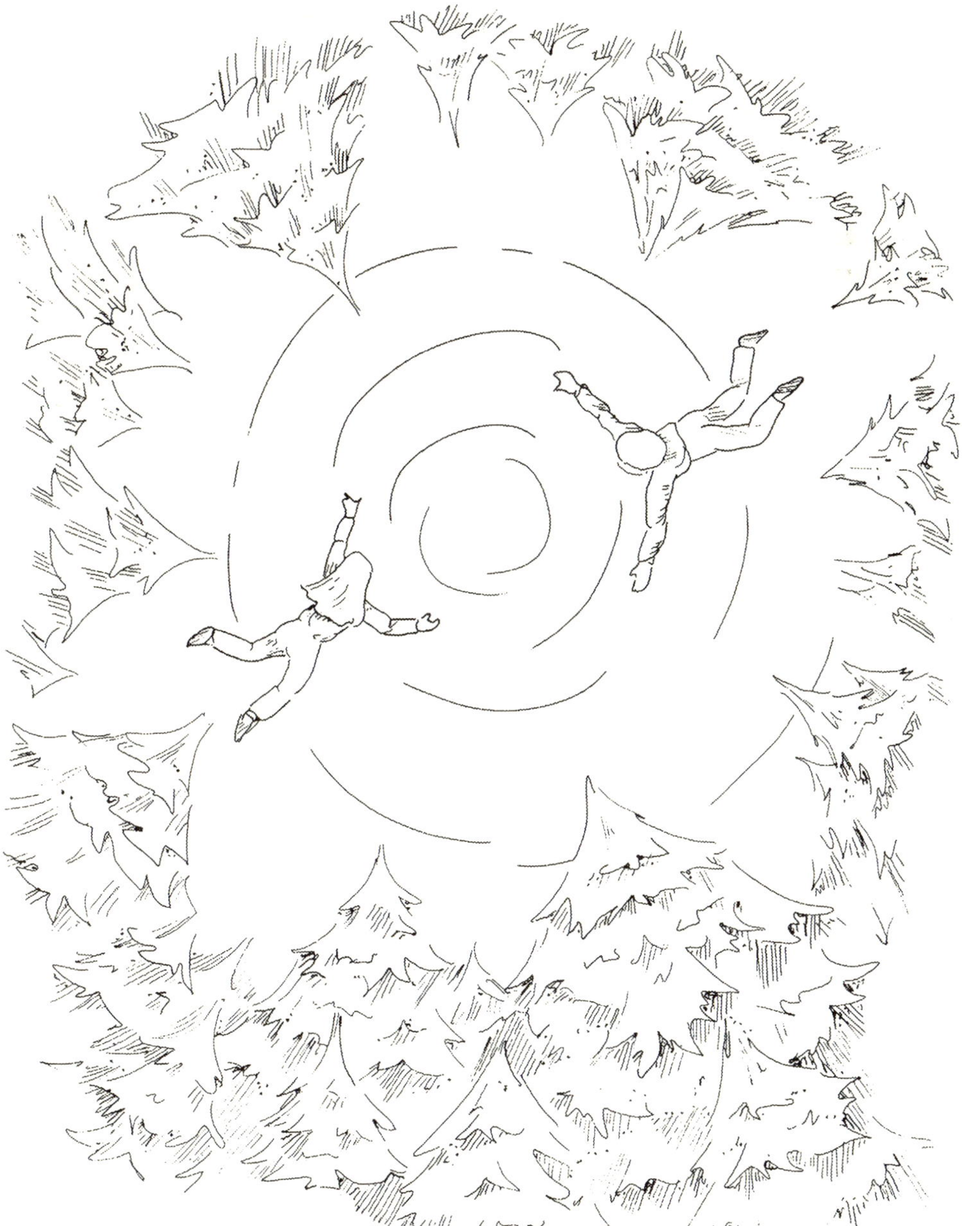

The Light of Love

"For unto us, a child is born." (Isa. 9:6 KJV)[20] And so it was ... the Father giving of Himself a child to be offered to humanity so they might have a chance to be free. This event literally changed the vibration of the world, for as this gift of Love was received and accepted by the people of the earth, they looked to God, their Father as being the Divine Giver and acknowledged His Light within.

Around the same time 2,000 years ago, there was a little girl who was born in a nearby village. Throughout her childhood, she had listened to many of the wise men speak of "the Man clothed with the Sun". She always remembered those conversations very clearly. She thought she would surely recognize this strange man if she saw him, for the Light coming through him must be as bright as the sun. Oh, how she hoped to be blessed with only a glimpse of him, even if she saw only a part of his face. As she grew older, she began to hear more stories and, although her family loved her very much and provided a warm and kind home for her, she knew she must leave, and find out the truth for herself. She left one morning before the sun had greeted her village. There was excitement in her heart, for she knew everything was all right and that she would finally be living a life she had dreamed about for so long.

It was many sunrises before she reached the place where she knew this gentle Man was. She had been following a glow in the skies and a warmth in her heart. Finally, one morning, as she climbed a small hill, she spotted a small gathering of people; and there He was, with all the Love of the Father, sitting amongst these few people. In the days to come, her visits became very frequent to that spot on the hilltop.

She observed a lot. She saw how He smiled and touched the children, and how He always knew who He was. She watched how He was received by all the people. Sometimes there were many who were cruel to Him. She felt so sad when she saw that happening. The words said to Him were thoughtless and so unkind. Did they not know "The Sun in Clothes" as she called Him? "Forgive them! Please, forgive them!" she always cried out in her heart to Him.

She did not know if He even knew she was there. Somehow she thought He was aware of her, but she could not be sure. She would awaken before sunrise and walk several miles with her heavy jug to a well which was the only one in the area. Then after filling it with water, she would walk to a very small shed where she had been drawn by the Light inside that building. Quietly, she would slip inside and place the jug of water on the ground by her Beloved. She did this for days, then weeks, without any selfish thought. No one saw her enter or leave. She would come back later in the day to collect her empty jug. She continued to walk to the hilltop as often as she could during the day to listen to Him speak. She always thought about her family. This man spoke about His Father so much. She wondered what kind of a father would send his son out into different places to be spit upon, ridiculed, to have stones thrown at him, and to be laughed at – what kind of father does he have – and yet He says that He is One with His Father and that "a greater love than that of His Father does no man understand." She really wanted to know more; to feel the same Love He spoke of. And what was meant by, "My Father and I are One.²¹" She perceived that something was changing inside – that she was expanding, as she continued to dream of God, her Father.

One morning, as she was coming from the well with her jug balanced on her head, she felt the earth tremble underneath her feet. Her jug began to sway, and it toppled down and shattered into many pieces, spilling all the water. She began to cry for this would be the first day she had not delivered water to this Man of Light. The vibration increased as she fell to the ground. The earth began to hum as the heavens parted, and joined in the Sound of Love. Suddenly, there appeared a beautiful shaft of Light coming directly down to touch the ground. She almost fainted as she felt more Love than she thought could be contained in her body. Was she going to explode? No sooner had that question been formed, than she beheld a beautiful figure – radiating inside the Light pillar. The Being of Light smiled and stretched His hands to her. She melted and knew everything about Him as their fingers touched. She could only say what came from her heart.

"Teach me about Love, oh Master of the Sun", she cried. And he replied to her heart, "Dear Soul, how can I teach any more about Love when you know it already. For weeks you have given me the Water of Life. At that same time, you have been giving God your heart. Go, and let the world know about the Love in your heart. For, many people will be changed by your presence. Wherever you go, I will be there; and where I am, so is my Father in Heaven who has sent me." The girl closed her eyes and found she could see more with them shut. This shaft of Light became brilliant. She was drawn way up high within it, following a very delicate living thread of Emerald Light. She kept being drawn higher and higher until she saw the Sun. She was taken inside, into the very center of the Sun itself. She recognized this as the Love she had been feeling all these years. A silent, steady, powerful Being of Love entered and she knew He lived in all things.

As she looked closer, she beheld the shaft of light with the Emerald Thread coming into the center of this Sun and leaving it. This channel of Emerald Light was never broken. It then entered into the Man who was clothed with the Sun, the Master of Light. His being increased in vibration as the shaft of Emerald Light radiated through Him and began to descend and enter into lots of little lights upon the earth. Many levels of life seemed to open, like petals of a closed flower, when they accepted this Light of the Sun into themselves. The worlds began to spin to the Sound of Love – radiating into the Heart of all Creation.

All that was sent forth from that point of Love within the very Heart of God, was given unto the hearts of men, freely, as a gift to help them know who they really were … Light Divine.

She could not seem to hear any more, and she simply fell asleep. When she opened her eyes, she found her jug repaired, and filled with the Water of Life. She lifted it gently onto her head and walked silently back to the shed, where she placed it before the Son.

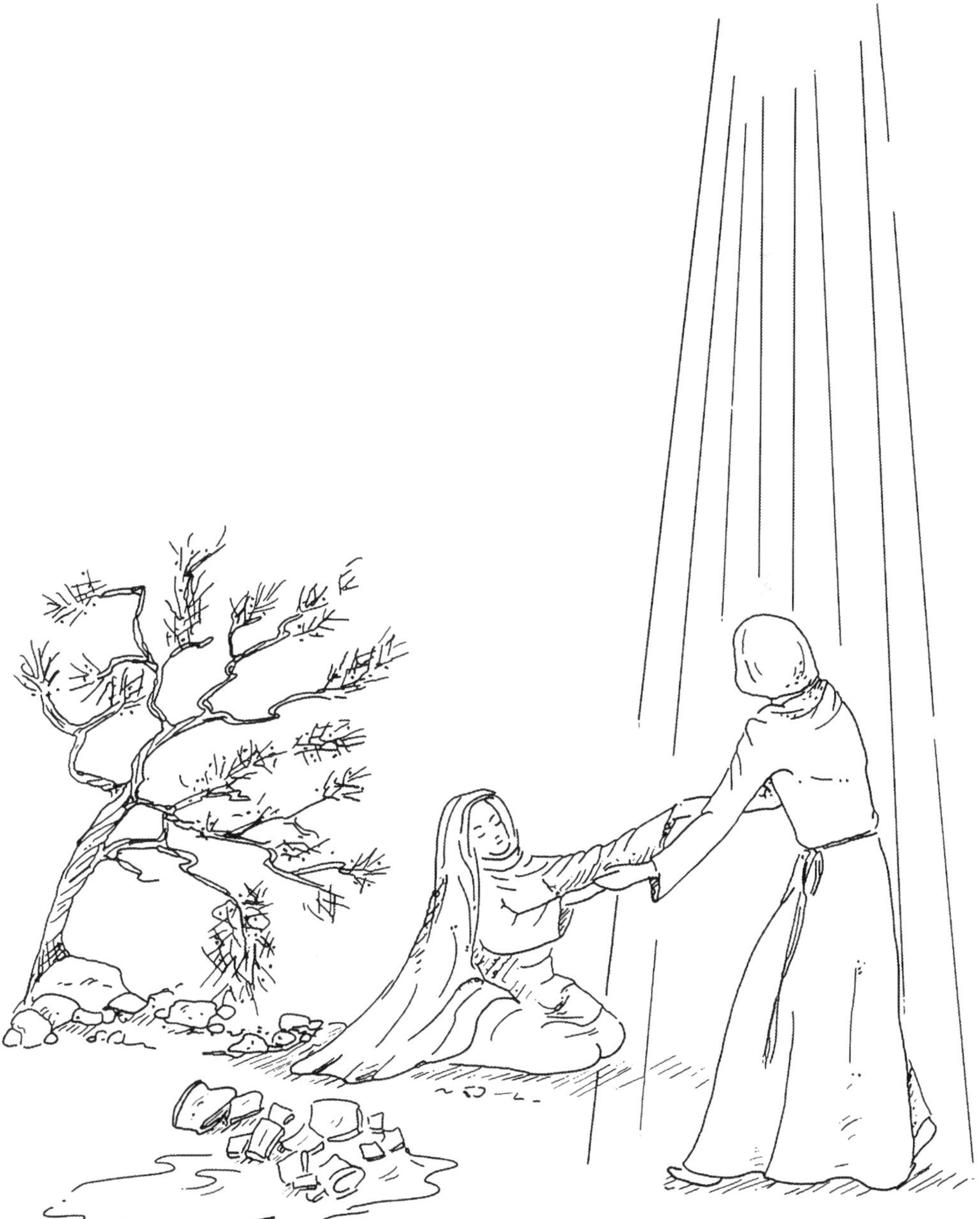

The Secret of Shalimar

Once upon a time, there was a people who lived very simply in the Land of Shalimar. The people of Shalimar were known as the "Keepers of the Sacred Simple Secret." They lived together, played together and worked together as One. In everything they did there was a sense of sharing and joyfulness. Throughout Shalimar there was peace and joy because each one held in their heart the Sacred Simple Secret.

If a visitor came from the outside, they could easily see the Secret by the sparkle in their eyes and the gentleness of their touch. To listen to them speak or merely watch them at play left one with a song in one's heart and a dance in one's step.

Now, there was one place where the Sacred Simple Secret could always be heard, seen, and felt. It was in a deep, deep cave in the very center of Shalimar. There lived an extremely old man who was said to chant the Secret over and over again, never ceasing, not even to eat or sleep ...

Down in the valley in the Children's School, one of the favorite topics of conversation was of the day when they would all go together to the cave. They knew that in order to hear the Secret, they would all have to learn to sit quietly. If they all concentrated upon being still and working together; then, perhaps they would all hear his gentle voice sounding forth the Sacred Message.

The children spent time daily practicing silence and meditation. They also spent time working together as a group. In all their activities, whether together or apart, they began to sense a closeness, a connectedness. They felt as if they were all a part of each other. The more they loved and cared for each other, the more this feeling of Oneness grew ...

One day, the teacher announced that the time was coming soon to visit the cave. An excited whisper rustled around the room. They all knew that the time was near at hand when they would see how well they had learned to work together. As the great day drew nearer, they practiced with increased dedication, knowing that this opportunity did not come very often.

One morning as the children gathered for their morning attunement, the teacher told them, "Today is the day we visit the cave." Suddenly the room was very, very quiet; then, gradually they began to stir, and then to gather the things they would need for the long hike.

They made a final rest stop just outside the cave at a crystal clear stream. Some drank and some waded until all were cooled and refreshed. Then they all entered the cave together carrying lanterns to light the way. In the very center of the cave there was a large open room. It was there that they gathered. The children all sat in a large circle and joined hands. They began to listen intently. Every cell of their being was alert to the Voice in the Stillness. Gradually the Voice could be heard chanting ...

"Listen children, children of Shalimar.
Here is the Sacred Simple Secret.
Treasure it always, carry it in your hearts.

For only there can it grow and blossom forth.
Be simple in your ways.
Think first of what you can give.
Always consider the needs of others before yourself.
Most of all, allow Love and Caring to guide your every footstep.
This is the gift of the Sacred Simple Secret.
It is the way of Divine, Selfless Love."

And then there was stillness once more in the great cave. Each one present was filled with peace and thankfulness. Then all together they began to sing forth a song of praise. As that song grew more and more beautiful, there came a great Light in the middle of the cave. It burned in the center of their circle with such radiance they could barely look upon it. As their song came slowly into stillness, they realized that the music continued, not by their voices, but by the ethers themselves. It seemed to emanate from the flame of Light.

As they all stood up, they again heard a Voice, now much stronger than before. It said:

"Children, my dear children of Shalimar, you now have learned to work together and to Love each other. Because of this, from now on a flame shall always burn in this Sacred Hall, lighting the way for all to see the Sacred Simple Secret of Shalimar."

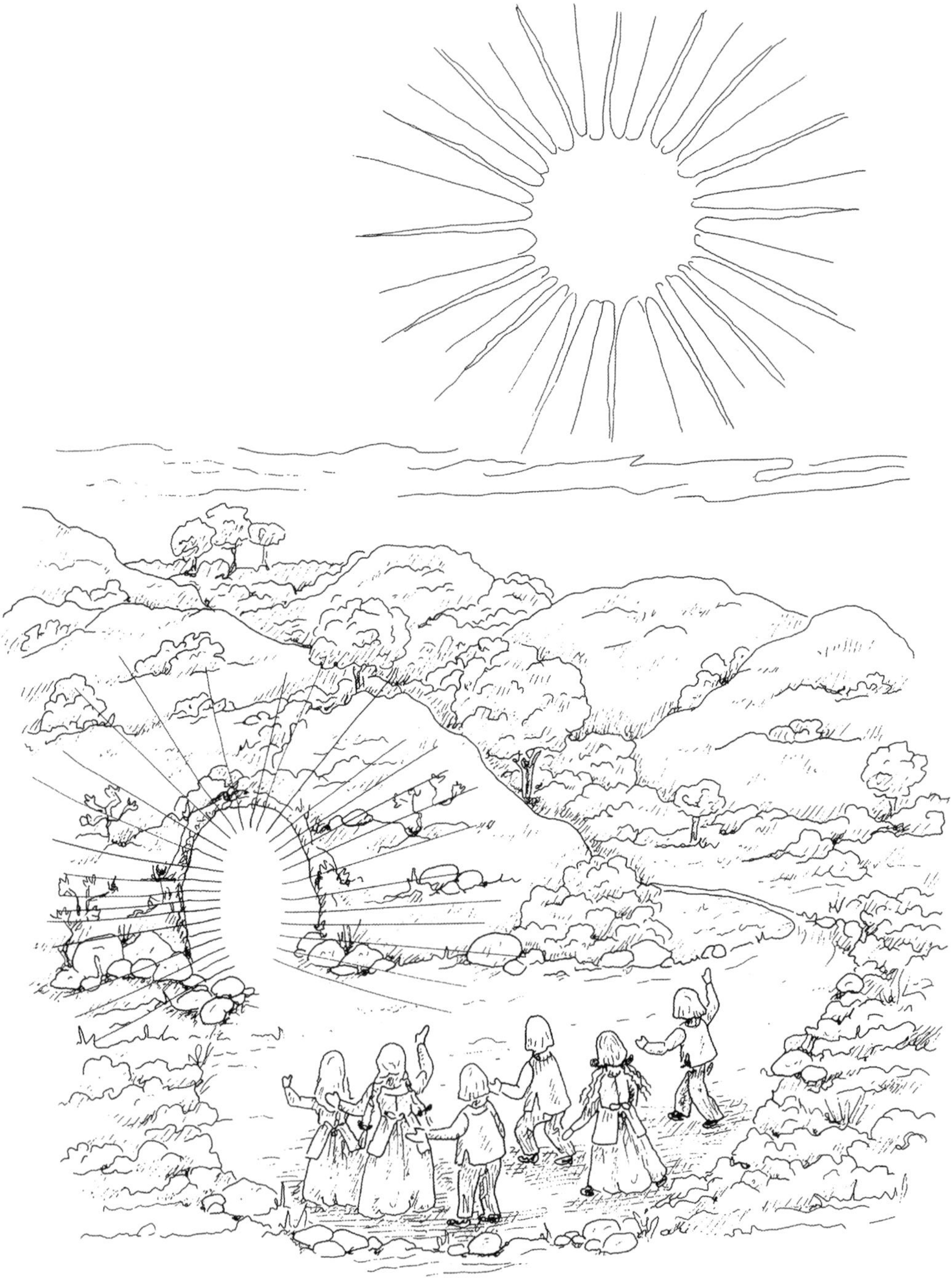

Love Ye One Another

In the beginning was The Word[22] ... and the Word was Love.

... It was heard throughout Creation: for it <u>was</u> Creation. The worlds began to form and to radiate the Light of Love. A song rang out sounding forth the angelic voice of Harmony and Peace. Swirls of colors danced and merged into one another. Love was everywhere. Love was everything. The constant pulsation of inhaling, exhaling was truly the breath of Creation – Love in manifestation.

On one tiny planet of blue and green brilliance, there lived a bright soul, whose heart was overflowing with the thought of Love in form and this new expression of life. For him, this was a time for expansion – for letting the Call of Divine Love pick him up and show him the wonders of Life. All was perfect!

But suddenly, a cloud began to cover this beloved planet of blue and green. The colors began to grow dull, and the sounds started to become muffled. This bright soul of Light found himself getting heavier and heavier. He thought, however, that if he tried real hard, he could still see the everlasting twinkle of Life smiling at him as he stared at his favorite walnut tree. But even that started to fade away, until finally, he forgot what he was even hoping to find when he looked at that tree.

The planet went through many changes over the years. And each time this bright soul came to this jewel of a planet, he was aware that his body was slower and his heart heavier. Life seemed to be getting harder. He didn't have much energy to do anything. There did not seem to be much meaning to circumstances in which he found himself.

Then one day, something very special happened to him. He was walking along a very dusty pathway, dreaming of the song of the birds, and trying to remember something he kept thinking he was forgetting. He suddenly stopped dead in his tracks. His eyes met those of a gentle-looking Man walking in the opposite direction on the same path. He gasped for his breath. This Holy Man of Light came closer to him and stretched out his hand, placing it on his chest, over the heart. The Holy Man greeted him with such incredible Love. This overwhelmed him so much that he felt his body suddenly go limp. His heart felt like the sides were being pushed open from the inside. Something happened! It was as if he was beginning to recall something. He didn't know what yet, but he knew he had to pay attention. Just then, the Light began to flood his Being. He saw himself standing in a whirlpool of pastel colors that went into him and through his body. He felt weightless and oh, so light. He began to hear that familiar Sound again, the constant whirring and humming of Love. Oh, how his Soul cried out to be set free – to love once again – to be ONE with that Light. For an instant, he remembered he was all those things and more. He heard the words which seemed to come from the voice of this beautiful Man he had just met, "Love God with all your heart, with all your soul, with all your mind, and with all your life.[23]" Those words resounded through his Being like a subtle explosion of pure Joy, and he knew, "God and I are One – One in Light – One in Love. We are One." The events in his life flashed before his inner eye, as he understood the touch of God in everything he did, in everything he thought. Now, how was he to live what he had been shown to be the Way? How? And the Man spoke again, "Love ye one another, as I have loved you.[24] Love ye one another freely." Once more, a wave of Light passed through him and he felt an inner strength taking over each cell of his body. Love one another in the same way God loved him. It was so simple. This strength to Love, where had it come from? He couldn't stop it from flowing through even if he wanted to, and he certainly didn't want to.

He opened his eyes and started to thank this glorious Man whom he had just met, but He had disappeared. Yet, somehow he knew all that he had just experienced made sense. He knew this Man would never vanish from his heart. His heart was still vibrating as he turned to follow the footsteps of the Holy Man into the Light.

If we love God with every fiber of our Being, we love everything. We cannot help but love one another. Our lives will change. We will welcome the challenges and opportunities to know more about Love in action, Love in form. Right now, we are being given the key to Love. We are being shown how to Love with an open heart. We are being shown Love beyond human pain and attachment: a Love Divine – one that does not hold or possess or expect anything in return. It is a Love that can truly set us free. If we accept this to be our time to know Love, we will ask for this key to be placed in our hands and it will be so. Our responsibility will then be to Love God and Love one another as we have only imagined possible in our dreams.

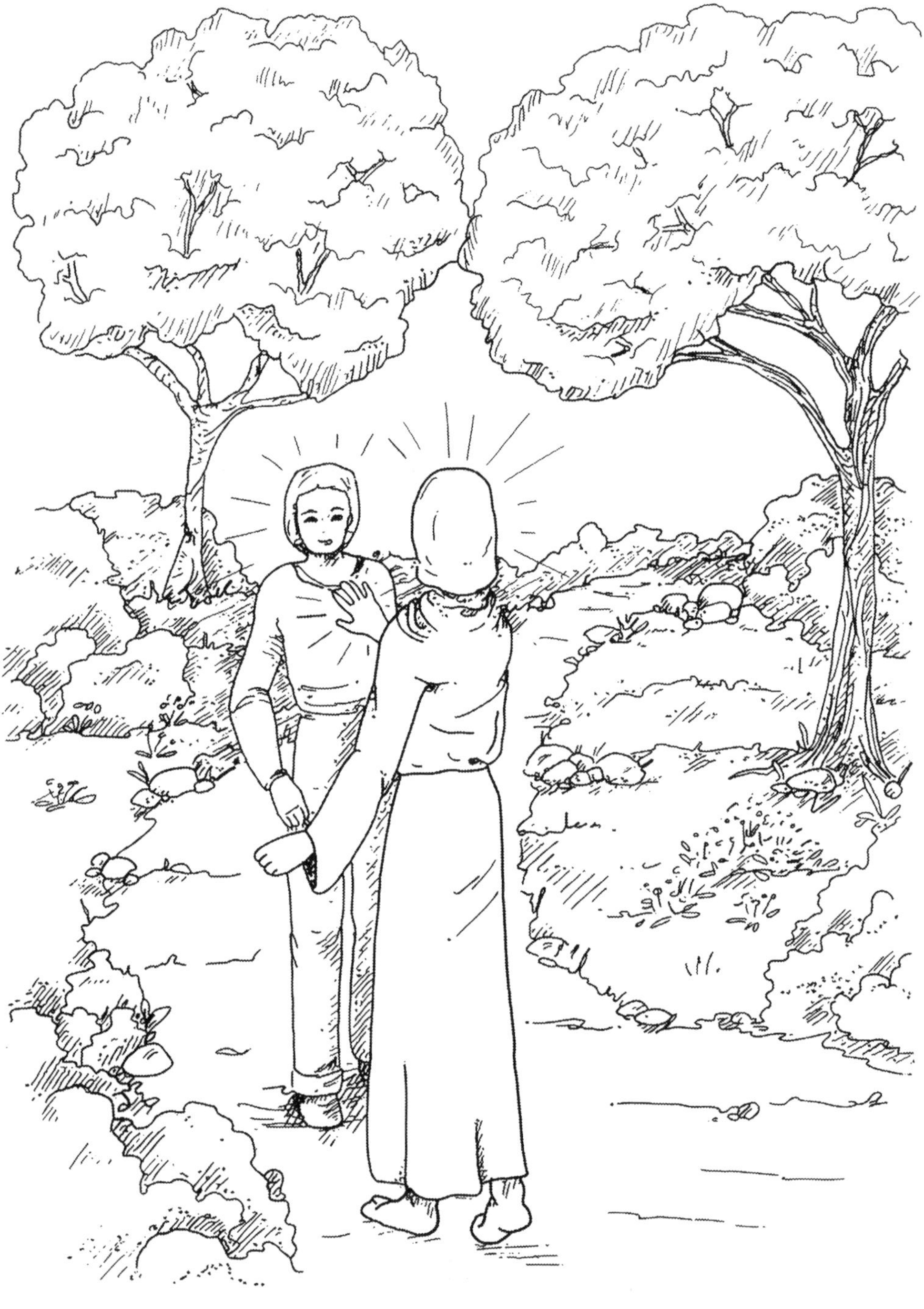

Steps of Joy

Mira and Teepal lived within a great crystal city which was almost transparent in nature. In those forms, they had never experienced any other place in creation. It was filled with the sound of angelic vibrations, permeating all substance. To limit the sound in any way would have been interfering with the perfect tonal frequencies heard by all, registering in the very heart of their souls. Teepal and Mira had always known they were One, even though they could move in and out of each other's space, for they knew it was meant to be that way from the beginning. They also knew that one day they would be leaving this crystal clear place and travel far away to experience the Love for their Creator in a slightly different form. This was an experience which was like an assignment for them.

The day came when they were finally ready for this adventure. They stood together, as one, embraced All, turned, and in an instant were gone from that space of pure Light and appeared in a totally brand new place. They were greeted by others who were living there already and were brought there because of their eagerness to discover and express that eternal love for God the Source of all.

Teepal and Mira spent many days acquainting themselves with the formalities and customs of this beautiful garden of Life.

It was a gorgeous place, filled with such unique fragrances and colors of incredible vibrancy. There were emerald green trees and multi-colored birds and flowers. A valley of such beauty and peace seemed to unroll right into a very pristine, pure mountain range. The beauty radiated the splendor of God's Love. And in response, the entire creation seemed to be singing a song, glorifying God's presence in all. It felt so much like Home!

One morning, Teepal and Mira found themselves walking on a small dusty path in the village. They thought they had heard some strange sounds and felt they were to follow them. After quite some time they stopped in front of a small shed-like structure. Opening the door, they beheld a tiny little child, all huddled up into himself, hungry, and cold and very much alone. They approached him gently and he screamed in fright. Teepal and Mira did the only thing they knew how to do. They sat with the child and sang to him – love songs to God. The melody began to calm the child and yet, just as peace seemed to descend upon the youngster, he would writhe uncontrollably or try to bury himself into the earth herself by frantically digging holes in the ground and trying to disappear into them. It was days before the little boy was ready to even look at Mira and Teepal long enough to connect with them in any way. Then one day, very early in the morning, just as the two were singing a most beautiful part of their eternal song, the child stood up and began to weep. All parts of him shook as he cried from the deepest part of himself, within his world. There he stood – frightened and alone. The two enveloped him with the calming presence of God and the little boy began to whisper to them with great pain: "I am, oh so cold. I do not know how to Love. I am so lost. Who am I? Why am I here? I am so alone. I do not even think I want to Love. Why does it hurt so much? Oh, I have forgotten who I am, help!" Teepal and Mira knew of this child's pain. They touched his heart with their glowing hands and instantly the child began to respond. A very small

Steps of Joy

flame of light seemed to ignite within the young boy's heart. It began to expand and glow from deep within – touching that changeless Source of Light – God. Just as the child was at the point of letting go totally, he glanced at Mira and Teepal. He was astonished at what he saw through the reflection in their gentle eyes of love, he beheld the vision of a child – a child who was so radiant. Instantly, the whole room was filled with words of love spoken directly to his pure heart of innocence: "Dear Child of God, there is no need to be afraid. For a moment in time you looked away but see now how the passion of your flame has been ignited. It was never extinguished. Let it grow. Yearn to Love God with all your heart, all of your being. It is then you will know of your original purity, your original innocence. It is there, within your heart, you will find all that is Real. It is not a path of hardship and suffering. It is a road of freedom – of peace and of divine joy. Trust your inner heart. Trust the Love you have for God. That will light your way, always. Go now, and remember: embrace each step – one at a time ... and may they truly be steps of joy." The young child stood there, filled with a feeling which he was beginning to recognize from So long ago. Then he felt himself move to the doorway of the shed he had been staying in for all this time. The door opened up – "Remember - let them be steps of Joy." Instantly, he skipped over the threshold and disappeared down the path towards Life, singing to the world: "Thank you dear God. I do love you so."

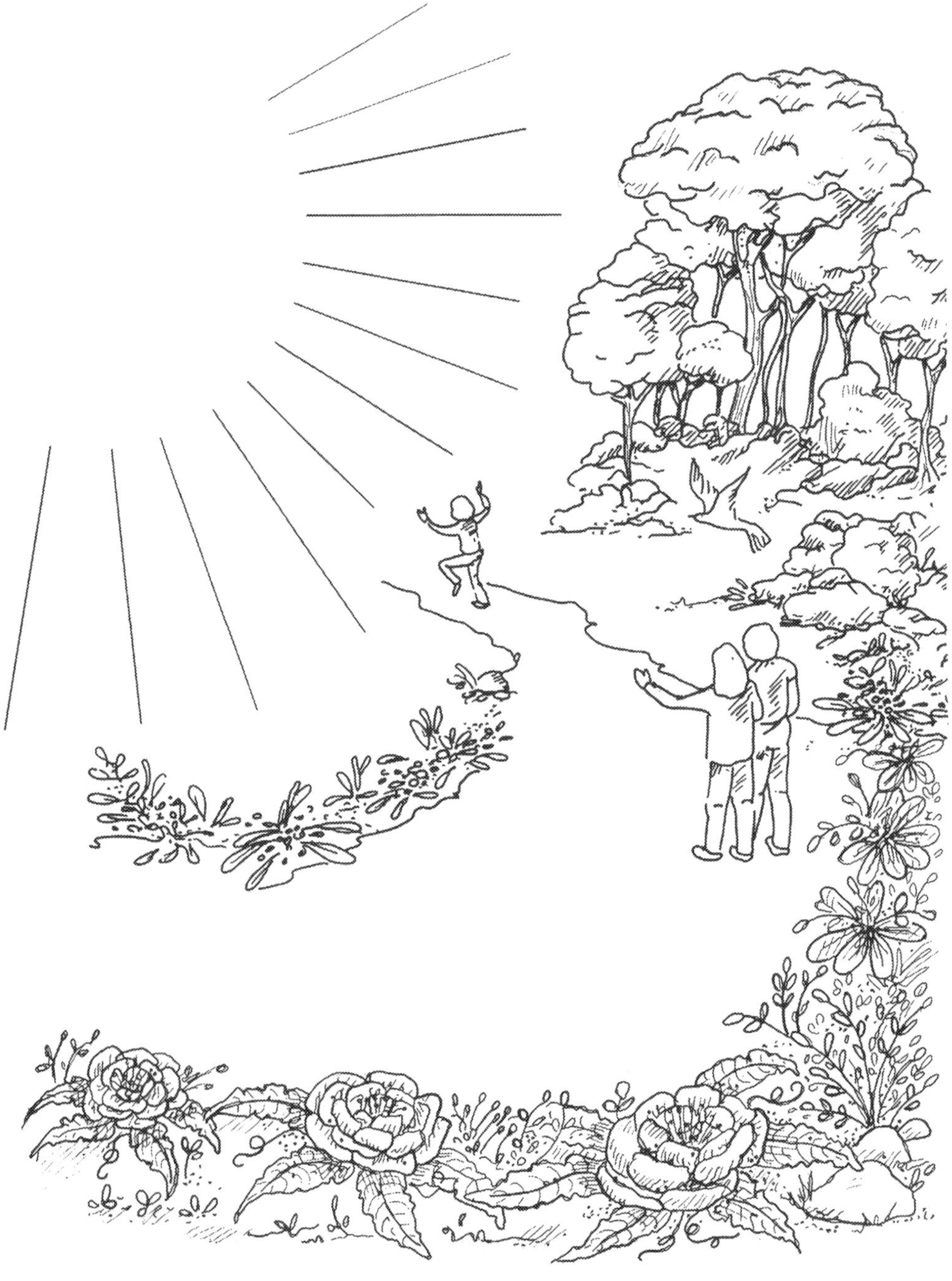

The Tinker's Gift

Once upon a time, in a very small village far away, lived an old man named Noah. He spent his hours quietly in his home or plying his trade as a tinker throughout the village. He would fix pots and pans, gadgets and tools, dolls, and spinning tops. It seemed that there was nothing he could not make as good as new.

One day, as he was walking down Sandy Lane, he saw a black and white kitten hovering in the corner by the market. The kitten appeared to be quite young and was soaking wet from the early morning rain. Noah picked her up and slipped her inside his jacket with loving hands but not a single word was spoken.

No one saw Noah for several days. Many began to wonder if he was ill, or may even have left town. The baker needed his oven repaired to make bread for all of the villagers. The candle maker's dipping pot had a broken handle, so he could not lift the wax over the fire and off again to make candles for everyone's homes. A crack appeared in the great bell in the bell tower in the center of town, so no one heard it tolling at 6:00, 12:00, and 6:00 again. They feared that the next ring might cause the bell to break. Mrs. Ansell's butter churn lost its handle, so there was no butter for her family. Many people started noticing all the things that the tinker had cared for, for so long.

Alas, weeks went by, and the villagers decided they must look for Noah. They went to his home, but no one answered when they knocked on the heavy wooden door. They looked through the fence beside his house and found to their amazement, the most wonderful courtyard they had ever seen. There were beautiful flowers in every color in the rainbow. They called out Noah's name, but no one answered. They opened the gate and entered the courtyard. The sweet smell of the many kinds of flowers filled the air. There were trees of every size and shape, and shade of green. They saw climbing vines and roses, a small pond, lined with carefully placed polished stones, and a beautiful marble birdbath where two robins were cooling off.

For a moment, everyone was silent as they feasted their eyes upon this small piece of Paradise, breathing in the freshness and purity of that air, and sensing all the love that was growing there. They were so involved with experiencing the courtyard, that they forgot why they had come.

Mr. Redova broke the silence as he called once more for Noah. Still, there was no answer. Again, they knocked at the door, but no one answered. Each asked the other what they could do. They decided to hold a town meeting to discuss the strange disappearance of the tinker.

That night, the entire town met in the town square under the silent bell tower. After much discussion, they discerned that Noah had last been seen with the black and white kitten early one morning several weeks earlier. A little more discussion and they all remembered how Noah had arrived just as mysteriously three years earlier.

The Tinker's Gift

It was a still, snowy evening three years earlier, that Noah arrived as the town was pondering how to get their supplies from Capitol City, for the mountain pass had become impossible to cross due to the heavy snows. After everyone had spoken, and no answer to the problem had arisen, the mayor called on the "thin, older gentleman in the back." Noah spoke up softly, but clearly, "Perhaps we could share what we have until the trip is possible."

Everyone agreed that, indeed, that was what they must do. And, so it was, that Noah was first remembered. From that day on, he offered to fix anything that was needed. Everyone in town had at least one story of a job the kind tinker had performed. He accepted food, or clothing, small homemade gifts, or a smile in payment as readily as he accepted money. No job seemed too big or too small for him to do. And each one was done as though it were the most important job in the world.

Everyone thought, and they thought, and they thought about what they could do. "If he returns, we must tell him how much we appreciate all that he did." "If he doesn't come back, we must build a monument to remember him." "We must care for his courtyard, for he loved it well." Then, a small boy spoke up and said, "We must care for each other, for he loved us well." There was silence. Then, everyone agreed, that the greatest gift they could give the tinker whether he returned or not, was to love each other as he had loved them and care for all the creatures who shared their village.

As everyone prepared to leave, a large black and white cat came running in. He jumped onto the boy's lap, and added, "Meow!" The town named him "Sunshine," and though he slept at the boy's home, beside him in his bed, the whole town cared for him, and remembered their beloved friend.

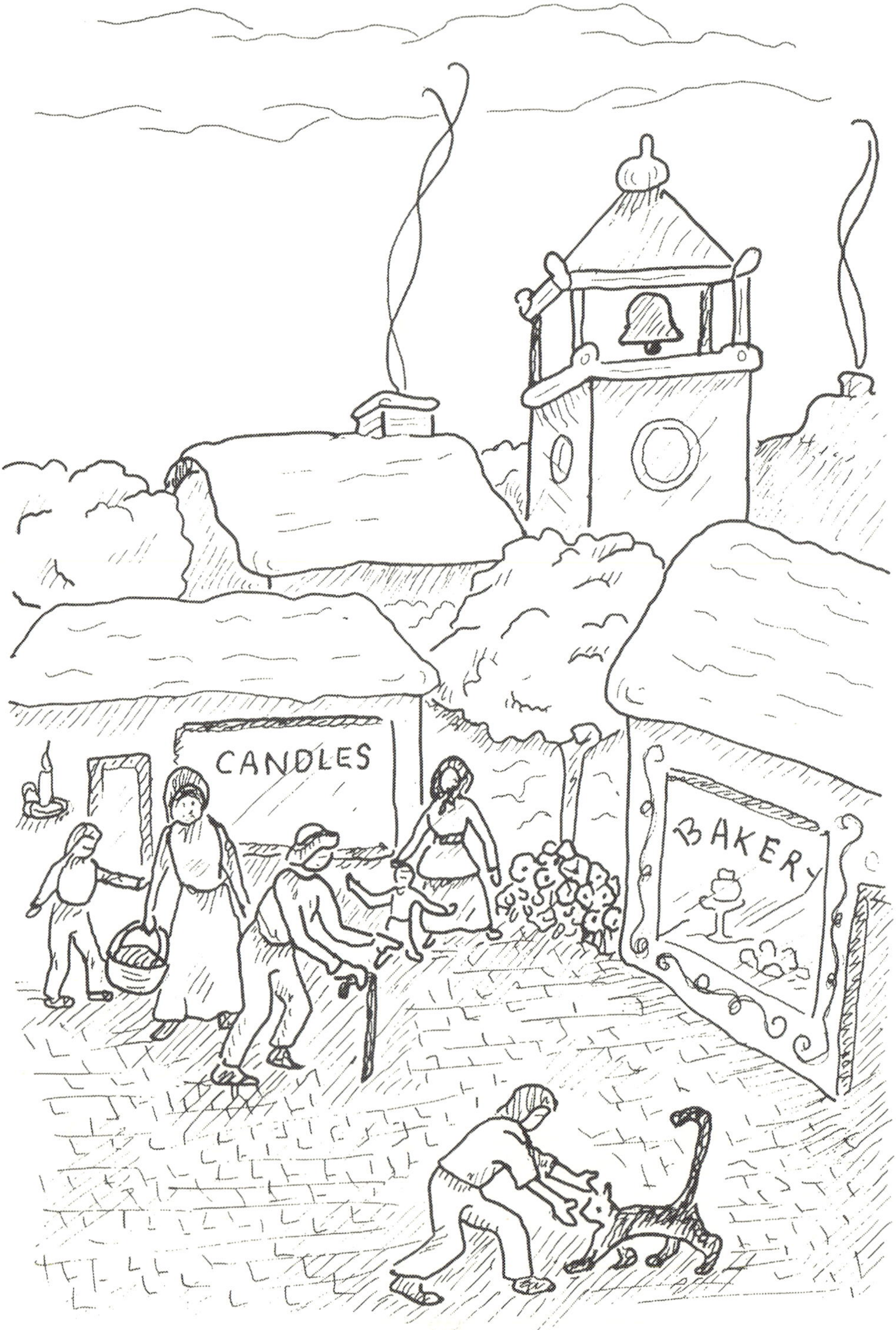
CANDLES
BAKERY

Lead Me to the Real

Lead me from the unreal to the real.
Lead me from darkness to light.
Lead me from death to immortality.[25]

The Upanishads

These words relay such a cry from the very depth of the heart. Inside all of us is the knowing of the real essence of Light, of God. Someday our search to know that reality will obsess our entire being and all our questions will begin to point us in the direction of our eternal home, in God. We would thus find ourselves fully awake. The inner search would no longer be one where we would be even thinking about receiving anything for ourselves in return. It would also not be a search based on our convenience, our available time. We would really discover it is an honest, sincere quest to know God, for His Glory, not so we could shine brighter as one of those who knows or has found the truth.

We have all had the experience of being at awe from witnessing and living the beauty of a sunset. Perhaps we watched the sun as we sat on the sand by the water's edge listening to the constant gentle sounds of the waves. Just as the sun disappears below the horizon, the colors begin to change. All around the glowing ball of light, there appears a living, pulsating radiance that seems endless. It penetrates the sky, the water, and most of all our hearts. It is as if the sun is saying to us, "Look, God made me. That is what you are seeing. It is the very same life-essence which is within you." Do we hear those words of the sun and want to know what they mean, or do we just see a beautiful sunset and feel emotionally uplifted? Does the experience add to the little world of our own experience and creation, or does it lead us to that which is real?

We find ourselves always having the choice of which world we wish to live in – the real or the unreal. We have invested so much time and energy into creating that which is unreal that sometimes we miss what is real altogether. Whenever we find ourselves in the center of our world, entertaining the thought of gain or profit for ourselves in any way, or just merely thinking about our own achievements, as noble as they might be, we have forgotten the very reason we are attending this important school of Life. We are here on this planet for the sole purpose to know God in full conscious awareness, to be absorbed in that knowing and then, like the sun, to radiate that pure light of love and truth, so that God might be glorified.

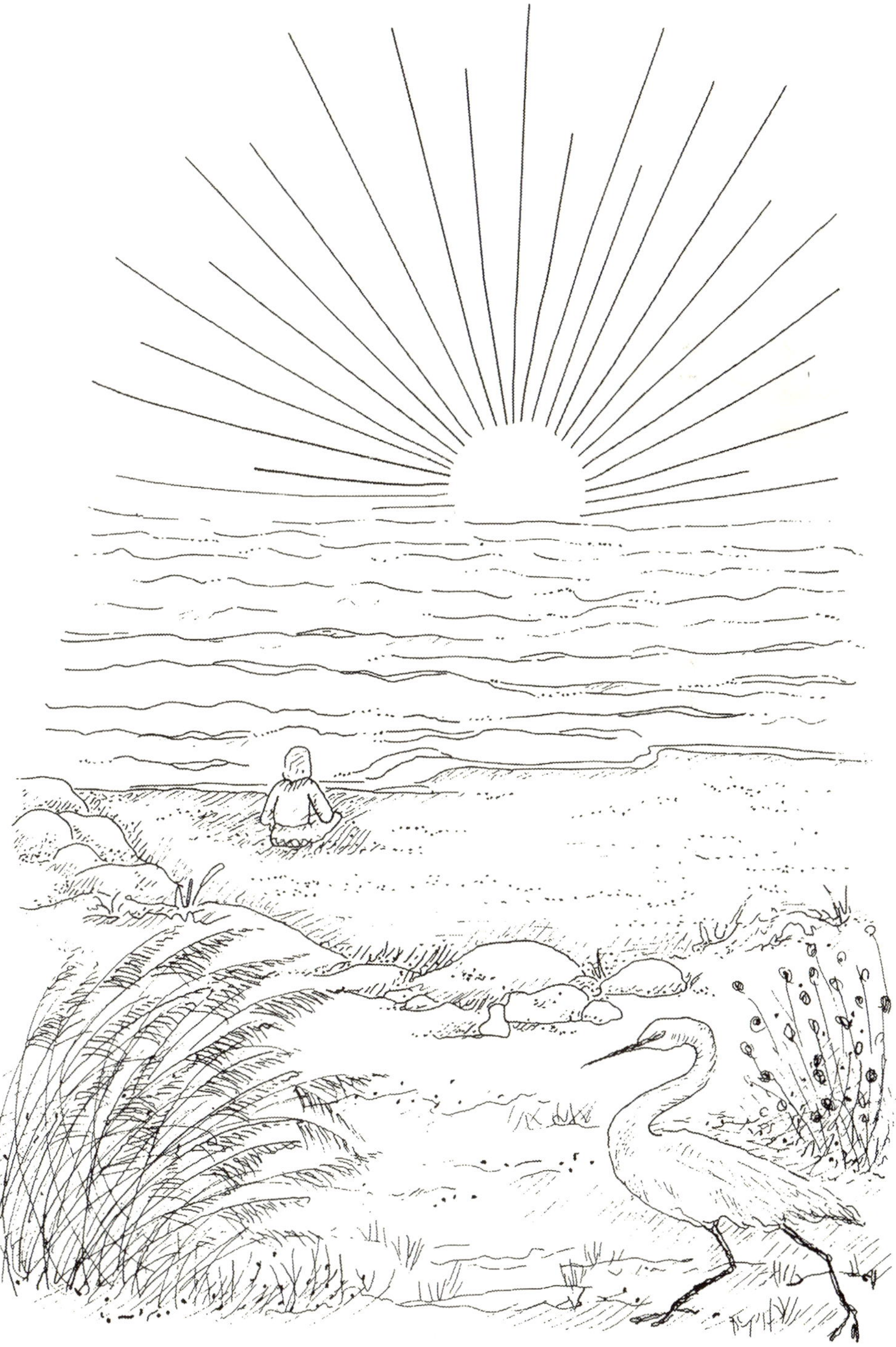

Paradise Found

Once, a very long time ago, there began to shine a Light, Emerald pure, around the beloved planet known as Earth. All things shook and trembled, and were awakened from a deep slumber. Many witnessed this change and were drawn there just to have the opportunity to play an active part in it. Those who got involved extended their hands to others along the way as they were rising to meet with the One Light of All. The earth opened more and was blessed with a Divine Being.

Time after time, as this Son, the Christ, was sent to the earth, He carried within His Being the complete vibration of that same Emerald Light. So filled with Love was He, that as He walked on the soil – the grass, the moss, the water – everything responded with exuberant love and joy to the sound of His gentle footsteps. Each time He came to teach, to be, to Love, He found those few souls who had come to prepare the way for His work to be done here on the earth. As He was a bridge to God, so were these small groups a bridge from the Emerald Light to the Christ vibration and then to humanity. The work of the Christ was to be kept pure throughout the ages and was to be passed from Light souls to Light souls. A silent mission of great importance was given into their caretaking.

One time, as the Word was sent forth through all creation that this Divine Being was to come once more to walk on the earth, there was a young boy and a little girl who both heard the vibrating message as a beautiful Being sang her song of prophecy to all the worlds. The children knew that it was true. The moments passed, until one day, they found themselves being drawn to a snow-capped peak … a place where the air they inhaled was as pure as the Light which they felt inside. The world certainly changed that day. What they met that day was a Being, clothed with the Sun, who touched their very hearts and softly spoke these words: "Oh, gentle Souls of Light, you are here to prepare for me my Father's Kingdom, so all may enter and be One; so all may know the Truth and taste of my Father's Love. May Peace be with all those who open their hearts to receive the Light of All. And most of all, dear ones, tell all those who care to listen, to Love God with all their beings, to trust Him to care for them and to Love them. Help them to first go within and find the Kingdom of God – the Light of All. Go now, we shall soon be together again, for he who serves God is One with me and I with him. Peace. Peace. Peace."

Yes, the two children knew that something had changed that day; and yet, they knew it would be a while before they were graced once more with the full touch of the Light. But their Joy far outweighed the sadness they felt. As the children grew, and when the time was right, they were brought together just to play and learn to love the Creator through each other. It was always so they could remember that dream which kept occurring to both of them each time the first snow fell in the winter.

The years passed until the words burned like fire in their hearts, "Prepare for me My Father's Kingdom." The trees resounded with those very words … each person whom they met reflected those words in their eyes. They could not escape what they heard. Finally, it was time for the words to blossom into expression. The earth was ready; the Being clothed with the Sun was ready. Everything was just right. People began to come together and love gradually opened their eyes. An opportunity to know the Light within was offered to all who wished it. Those who responded might have been few but always enough. And, so it went: first silently, and then with more outward expressions. The word was spread: "Let go and let God manifest in your life. Be One with the Light of All. Be still and know that I Am God.[26] I AM ... LIGHT. Go within and seek the Kingdom of God first.[27] Now as One, let us prepare the way for Him who has come to bring Light into the world of shadows."

The message is always the same. Even now, this very day, there are those who have gathered in response to the Call. The time is now. Let us live the Kingdom of God here on earth, so all may know what it is. Let the Light of the Kingdom within radiate, and let it be our gift of Thanksgiving to God for giving us the understanding of His very life – Love Divine.

Paradise is found ... There is a place where all souls can come together as One and merge into the Light. The teachings, kept pure from the beginning, are being taught, as the way is being prepared for even greater things to be done. May His Will always be done in us and through us. We are ONE!

Truth is the Way

Truth is victorious, never untruth.
Truth is the way; truth is the goal of life,
*Reached by sages who are free from self-will.*²⁸

Mundaka Upanishad

What is that unique element that suddenly comes alive inside of us and exclaims from deep within that it is time to let go, to relinquish our self-identity and all the numerous games which maintain us in a confused and separate state, far from recognizing our true Source of being? Sometime we will come to the point when our search to know and love God with all our hearts, our minds, our very souls will be so all-consuming that there will be no room left for our self-created world. Our experience on this beautiful planet holds so much for us. It offers us an opportunity to know freedom, to manifest Love and to let go of the erroneous concept that we are alone and separate, not only from each other but from God. We have the chance to know God's Love for us and for all creation, and to thus open to what Teresa of Avila termed "real humility". She understood that state to be one of simply recognizing that God knows us better than we know ourselves and that all that is offered to us is for our own good. All the challenges and experiences He brings to us each moment of the day are only there to allow us the chance to see what is real, thereby letting go of our self-defeating world and relinquishing the unnatural need to build our separate identities, as glorious as they might be. When Teresa talked about needing to be satisfied with what God brings to us in the form of experience, she was not referring to just tolerating it, but rather to embracing and welcoming everything into our lives, recognizing that He truly does know us more than we know ourselves. Therefore, all the ingredients for our ultimate freedom are in place. We merely need to accept the invitation to be free.

For this, we need to cease projecting onto an experience our own past concepts or planned expectations of how it should be or what we are to be learning from all of this. That process of projection and expectation is a sure way to close the door to knowing. Where is the freedom of life, of truth, of God's presence? It is really a great leap of faith and trust which we must make when we are facing letting go of the precious concepts which preserve and protect our own kingdom. How proud we might be of our own world, our creation, especially if others believe it is wonderful, too. When do we finally say, "Stop! This serves no purpose anymore. I want to be free, not a slave to my own self-created world. I want out!" This does take a lot of courage, as all the ancient mystics have related to us. And, it is true, that this inevitable step can only be made by the brave of heart, seeing all creation as a friend, filled with the Life of God, beckoning us to let go and follow our heart's calling to know and live what is real and true.

Each time we take a step in the direction of letting go of illusion, of the unreal and of our false separation, we are filled with a greater knowing of our eternal love for God. Finally, we find we cannot resist anymore. We freely lay down and relinquish our self-will, not as a sacrifice, but as a loving step toward freedom – to merge with the One divine will of God. Yes, Truth is the goal of Life.

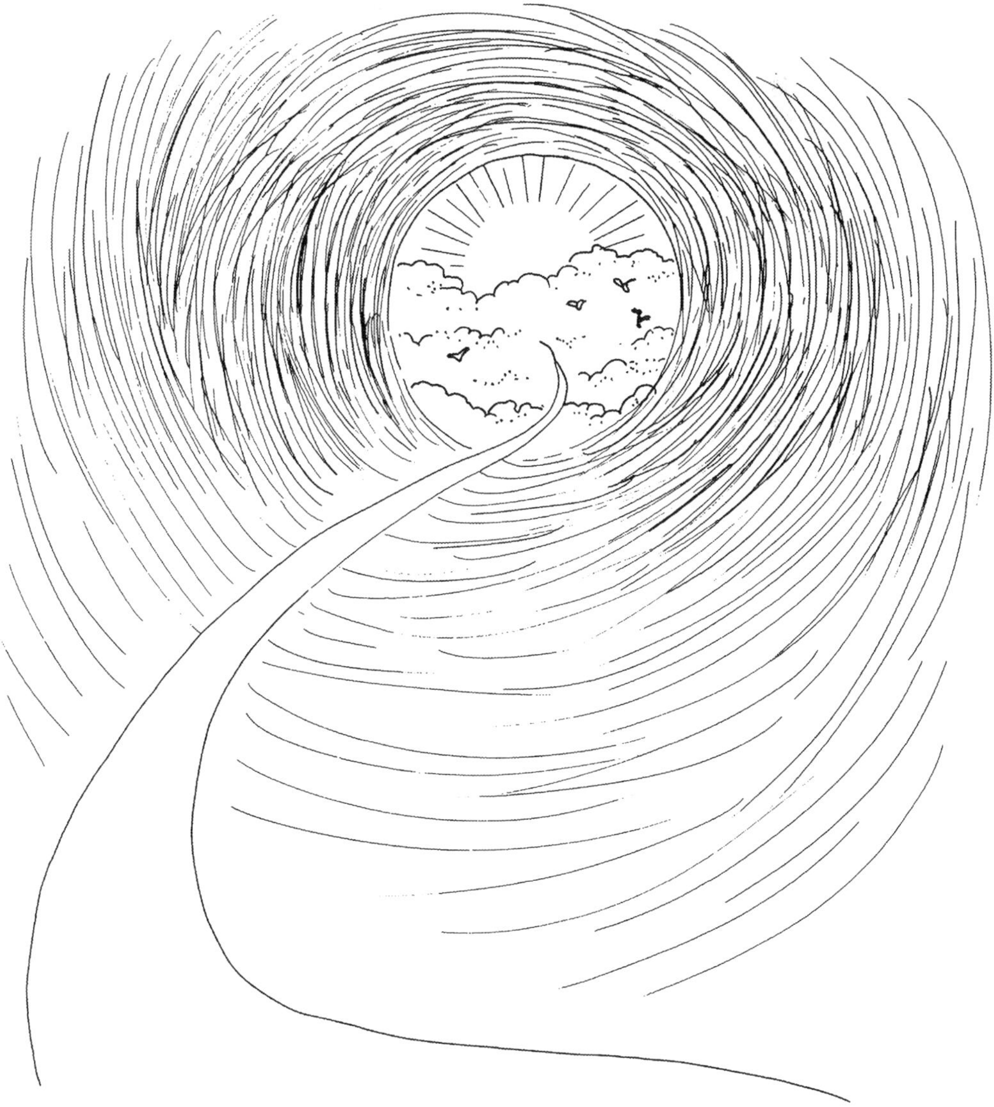

Once There Was a Man

Once there was a dream hidden deep within our hearts. It was a dream of the kind of life we had never seen: a life of peace and joy and love, a life where all people were happy and cared for and free. A life of an abundance that could never be diminished, but was continually replenished as quickly as it was used; a place of unimagined beauty, a Home …

A man came along who spoke to us of such a dream, which he too shared. He called it the "Kingdom" and promised us that it was not only real; it was at hand. We would have laughed at him, but there was something about him – something about his eyes, his face, the way he carried himself … we did not laugh … He stirred something within us, even in those who opposed him and came to hate him. There was something about him.

Word of this man began to spread, and as it did, hope was kindled in the hearts of the people – a hope that they had not known in long ages of suffering. Like wildfire in the dry season, rumors flashed wildly about. Words were used about him, strange words: "messiah" … "the holy one" … "God's son" …

We watched him as he worked in the heat of the day; we watched him eat in the cool of the shade. We began to follow him about when we could. He would speak to us – sometimes of this "Kingdom" ... sometimes of working with wood ... sometimes he would stop what he was doing to play with the children, a most unusual man.

Then, his travels began, and we never saw as much of him as we would have liked. Whenever we heard he was returning; there was great anticipation and joy in our hearts, though we were not sure why. Yet, when he did come, there was also a trembling, and some of us were afraid to look upon him in the face; yet also afraid to look away ... There was something about him ... the priests hated him; the soldiers mocked him; the children adored him. We were in awe of him.

Somehow our lives were changing. The way we felt about things, the way we behaved toward one another ... Something was stirring inside us, and we began to believe: perhaps there was a "Kingdom" after all. Perhaps he would take us there. Once, a great leader had led our people away to a promised land. Would he lead us so again? ...

It was difficult for us openly to admit our new and wondrous belief in the face of so much adversity and mockery, for we all wanted to be well-liked. Surely we weren't taking him seriously, people would say. All we knew for sure was, our lives were not the same as before he came. We had begun to care for one another more; and, strangely enough, had likewise begun to have more faith that we were cared for. He spoke to us of a "Father" ... our Father ... His and ours ... all of us. And something in our hearts leapt for joy. There was so much to fear around us, but somehow it all just seemed to fade away in his presence. We began to feel a strength, from deep inside ...

One day, there were shouts among the people and a great clamor arose. There was much confusion and there were throngs of people everywhere. No one seemed to agree about what was happening, but something powerful was definitely in the air. Then we heard, and we ran up to the hillside, approaching as close as the soldiers would allow. Three men hung there, naked to the world, and dying ... And there we saw him, in the center of the other two ...

Our hopes were crushed, and our hearts felt as if they had just been broken. None of us could speak. We could only watch in mute disbelief. This was our prophet, the Holy One of God? ... What of the Kingdom he had promised? What had become of the dream? So we were fools after all ...

We were about to leave, it was all too much to take; when I heard him say: *"Forgive them, Father, for they know not what they do ..."(Luke 23:34 KJV)*[29] As we turned, he raised his face toward us, and in his eyes was the greatest love we had ever seen, and we burst into tears, and slowly, we began to understand. This was not where the dream ended, but where it began. This "Father" he had taught us of, was not ours alone. He was the Father of us all: the soldiers, the priests, everyone ... Somehow, this one man had known that, and he, like His Father, had loved them all. Perhaps this was the Kingdom, this love so great that not even pain or death can daunt it. Perhaps the Kingdom was Love.

You need not seek God here and there: he is no farther off than the door of the heart. There he stands and waits and waits until he finds you ready to open and let him in. You need not call him from a distance... Your opening and his entering are but one moment.[30]

Meister Eckhart

The Minstrel

Once upon a time, a young man sat down to pray. He was tired and sore and more than a little afraid. And so he asked, "What is it all about? Who am I?" ... No answer came. Only the Silence remained. So he traveled and studied far and wide in his quest for answers, until he became, oh so wise. People sought him out for counsel, and he responded with warmth and pride. Many were the talks he gave and the books he'd read, but at night, alone in his bed, his heart was still filled with dread. And his shoulders grew bent from the weight -- not of his years, but of his inner tears.

One day a woman who knew him well told him his greatest work was his music and the songs that he sang. And he had laughed -- for they were such simple things, no master of the craft was he. But as time went on, even the music wouldn't come; for though his head was filled to bursting, his heart was as empty as a drum.

He prayed again, not in words but in his Being: "Oh God, is this the pain so many feel; is this what it means to live apart from your Love? ... Then please, help me. Give me a song again to spark their hearts and lift them from this misery. Help them. Help their hearts be filled with the song of your Love ..." And no answer came. Only the Silence remained ... And then it

AWAKENING – A Journey Within

began to burn, and burn and burn until it burned him to white … until there was nothing left of him but Light. And then the Music came -- not from him, but from the very Heart of God. And he sang and sang and sang -- not just with his voice but with His Being -- and all who heard were healed. And the only voice that could be heard was that of his own heart: "Thank you, my dear God … thank you forever and ever …"

The Year of Acceptance

This is a new year, a time to celebrate life and to truly accept all that is real and alive within our very being. How do we go about doing that? John of the Cross, Kabir, Teresa of Avila and so many other passionate lovers of God knew that in the end, we could not induce or create a knowing of that reality within – not even a small glimpse of it. They all said repeatedly we must just let go of all self-identity, self-centeredness and accept to be absorbed in the One changeless Source of all life – God. We must merely embrace God with all our hearts, accepting and allowing Him to gently fill us with His Love and thus guiding us back home to Him, where we would surely discover we never really left.

What is it really that we are on the threshold of accepting? Is it not our true nature? Is it not the greatness of Spirit-within? Will acceptance of Reality change our lives? How could it not! We would have to let go of the building of our own illusions – all the planning of "getting ahead" and succeeding within the littleness of our confined worlds. Letting go, surrendering that which is no longer serving us anymore – how could that be a sacrifice, when all we risk to lose is what we have built? When we let go of competition, judgment, criticism, our perfect image, and our success in the eyes of the world, what would we have left? Reality. God.

Certainly, we would know freedom in a very different way. What allowed John of the Cross, Teresa of Avila, Gandhi, within their awakened consciousness to traverse the abyss between the yearning souls and the union with God? Did they possess some magical element that we do not have or that only is reserved for the very few? They would have cried out from within that we are indeed all the same, and that the same ache is within all creatures – within us all. So, what was it that gave them courage to stand up and pursue the vision of their heart? If it is in us – then why is it so hard to find that special veiled element that unlocks our heart's desire? It is within us all. As John of the Cross wrote, *"How gently and how lovingly Thou wakest in my bosom.[31]"* Something comes alive inside that literally transforms our lives. Concepts begin to change. Instead of being scared to face what is not real, there is a desire and strength that is ever-present as we open to what is real and to let go of what is not. Recognizing God is the only thing that exists within our heart, and accepting His sweet breath of Life, we so totally lose ourselves and are absorbed in His gentle swirling column of Love – never to desire to be separate again – even for a moment.

We may begin by wanting to know the Divine Will of God within our own worlds, but eventually, we awaken to the realization that to know His Will we must accept to let go of our worlds and not feel that anything given to us is an obstacle to be overcome on our journey home. We must accept that all elements offered within our lives are potential keys to freedom – that God is calling us to be absorbed within His Heart of Divine Love, the Holy of Holies. Yes, this is a new year. Let us embrace it as a Child of God – freely, with Love in our hearts. Let us dare to open to accept God, full of grace and glory, and to allow Him to fill us tenderly with His Love forevermore. So be it.

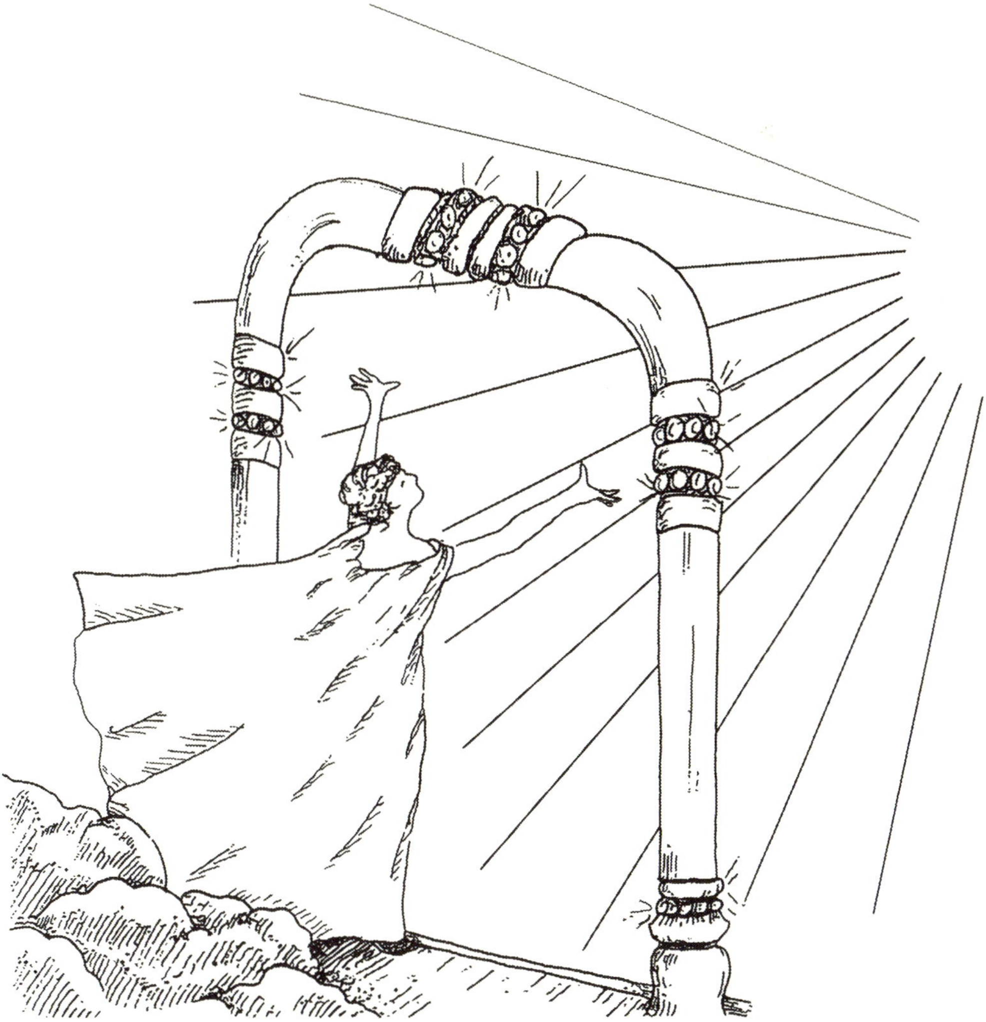

Proclamation of Peace

Oh, children of Earth, pay heed to these words of Love. Let your hearts stand open as Peace fills your beings. There is but so much time to ready the planet to accept the Love that is being offered. Each one has to do his or her part ... to be honest with oneself, to begin to live from the Center of Light, to live a life of Love, of peace. As one person on the Earth truly lives consistently a life of Peace, other hearts may be touched. Soon others will follow. Let this be a world which is filled with Love. This life of Light is for all nations, all peoples, all life forms. It knows no boundaries. It knows no limitations. Come join with those Beings of Light already manifesting a life of harmony in its fullest expression. The opportunity is for now. What will be your answer? May the Peace and Light of The Infinite One be with you now and forever more.

Peace on Earth

Why is it so hard to learn to live in peace? Why is it that every nation today is either at war or threatening war against other nations? Why is it that people today find it so hard to live together in peace, harmony and love? How did humanity get to this point where it is on the verge of self-destruction? What brought this about?

A very long time ago, even before the creation of this planet, there was a Divine plan, an idea of what this world was to be. It was to be a beautiful, lush garden where all Beings were to live in peace and harmony, knowing that they were all an integral part of the Divine Light from which they had emerged and to which they would return. The Creator of this planet had given the responsibility to a designated group of "Sons of God" to be caretakers of this beautiful garden. This would work very smoothly as long as all these caretakers would keep their eye focused on the One Light – the Creator of All.

Because of the selfishness of some of them, the Light dimmed in the garden, and progressively peace and harmony disappeared. As a result, the planet with all of its beautiful forms took on a density not previously known. Other "Sons of God" were sent to work on uplifting this sad situation back into the Light. Throughout history, some of these Beings appeared as prophets or seers. More often than not, they were persecuted or put to death. A promise was made from the beginning of this sad happening, that periodically, throughout the unfoldment of this planet, Beings of magnificent Light would come and break this shell of darkness and open a path for all, back to the Divine Source, back to the Light.

One of those times when the promise was fulfilled was two thousand years ago. The Creator of All, the Source, sent to this planet a Pure Being of Light clothed in Love. This great Light was not sent to die, but rather to live in the form so that we would have life and have it in abundance. He came to restore the Divine plan, to show the way to the Kingdom of Peace, Harmony and Love. He came to stimulate the memory of times past – where brothers and sisters lived together, were kind to one another and cared about one another. Thus, there was a chance to see the perfect Plan of the Kingdom manifested in form. This beautiful Being of Love never judged anyone for the planetary situation of his time. He merely loved all humanity without limitation, for He understood that they had forgotten, and did not know of their true heritage and their Divinity. For if they did, surely they would have chosen Peace, not war, Brotherhood, not separation, and Service, not selfishness.

As we reflect on this message of Love brought two thousand years ago, we recognize this as the same message going out from the Heart of God right now to all of us. He is sending out invitations for laborers to build the Kingdom of God. *"I call you friends because I have made known to you everything I have learnt from my Father. You did not choose me. No, I chose you, and I commissioned you to go out and to bear fruit, fruit that will last ... What I command you is to love one another." (John 15:15-17 TJB)*[32]

We do make a difference. We can go out and bear fruit and love each other. We are the Children – the Children of Light ... and this planet can be that beautiful garden of Peace and Love it was meant to be. It has to begin somewhere. So, let it begin with us – each of us who chooses to be a part of the answer and not part of the problem – each of us who would open to love one another as the Christ loves us. May this be the time in the evolution of the planet where men and women stand for Divine Freedom, Universal Intelligence and Unconditional Love. And finally, may this be the time that Harmony and Peace will reign on earth forevermore.

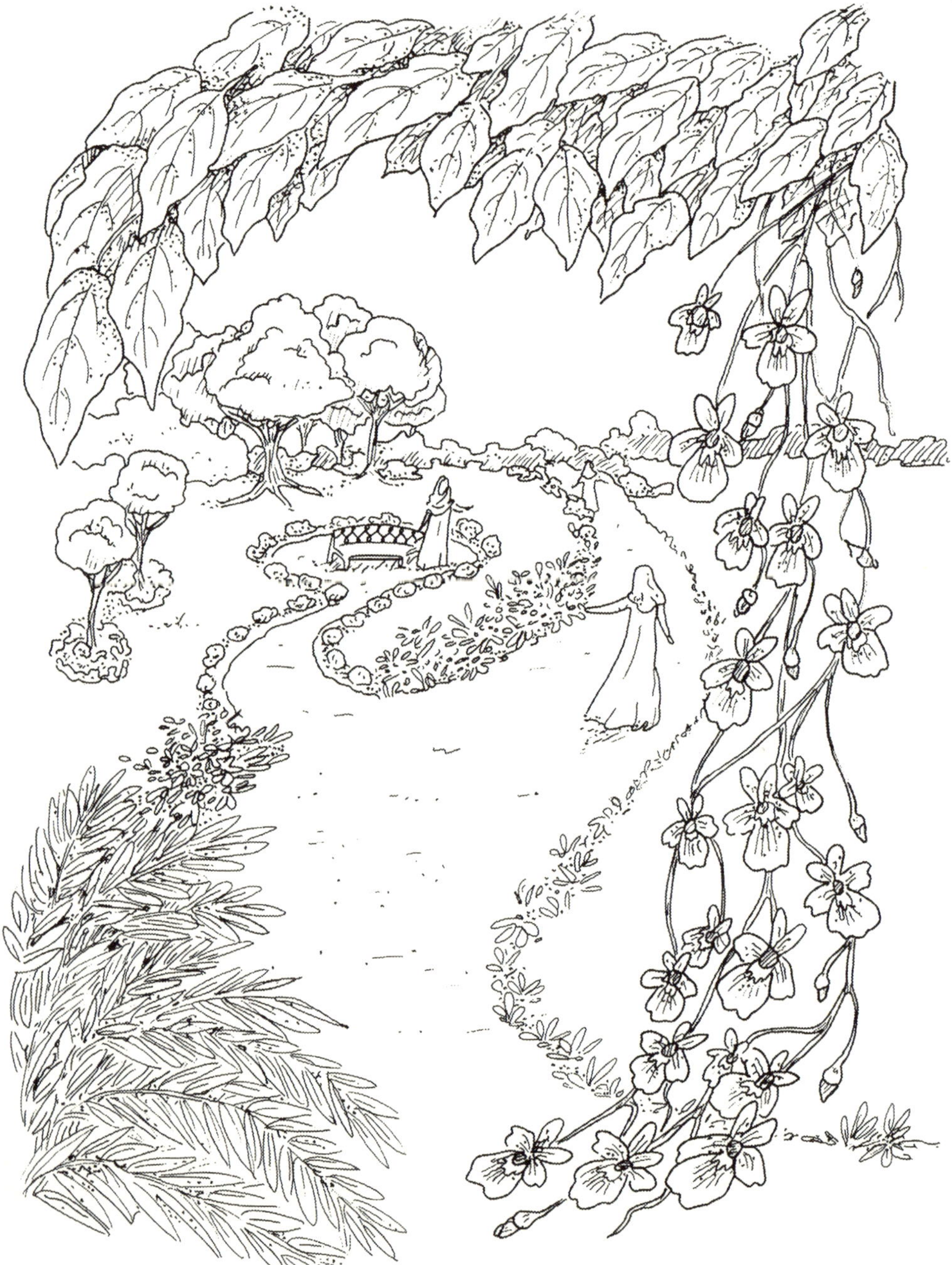

Loving God is All There Is

I never ask God to give himself to me. I beg him to purify, to empty me. If I am empty, God of his very nature is obliged to give Himself to me to fill me.[33]

Meister Eckhart

Springtime, what a magical time of year! Can we not hear the passionate exclamations of love that all the trees are singing as they shimmer in the sunlight? Do we not see the courage and determination the little crocuses exhibit as they poke their heads out through the earth? What is it about this time of the year that we suddenly feel more alive and vibrant? It is certainly an opportunity for us to come out of ourselves, to wake up to a greater understanding of what we are here to experience and live on this beautiful planet. How free it is to discover we do not have to have all the answers beforehand for the many questions which are in our hearts. Those answers will only be known truly as we open to letting God live them within us. At that very moment, we will know! But what is that part which really knows? Is it not the God-within us which simply recognizes God? For it can only be God-nature which knows God-nature. Oh, how words seem to fail us at these moments as God touches our very souls, the inner depth of our being which belongs solely to Him.

Many of us have taken a walk deep into the beautiful woods where we might have found ourselves so overcome with a feeling of being one with all of nature. At that moment we are so empty of ourselves that we can lose ourselves totally in the wispy blade of grass or a soft clump of emerald moss. We might discover very suddenly and certainly unexpectedly that we have woken up from a deep sleep and have found ourselves totally full of God. This is precisely what is so magical about Spring. It is as if it is pushing us to empty ourselves of our private separate worlds of littleness. While everything is shouting Life – it is very difficult to remain asleep and stagnant.

If we have courage enough to embrace each moment God offers us to live, we will find ourselves one with God swimming in a living, eternal ocean of Love. We cannot make any of this happen – for then all this would certainly be about us. We must simply lose ourselves in our love for God. Then we will surely find our true Selves – One with God bathing in His very essence. This is not impossible. It is inevitable, for this is truly who we are. It does take courage of the heart, persistence, and determination – not fear and tension. But most important of all is our love for God. That will ignite the flames of passion and rekindle the heart with courage. Just as the little crocus, with all its determination, yells from within its heart of beingness, "I am made to bloom God's colors, to love God completely and to radiate God's essence," so it is with us as we pop our heads out of our self-created worlds. We too are made to love God. So, let it be.

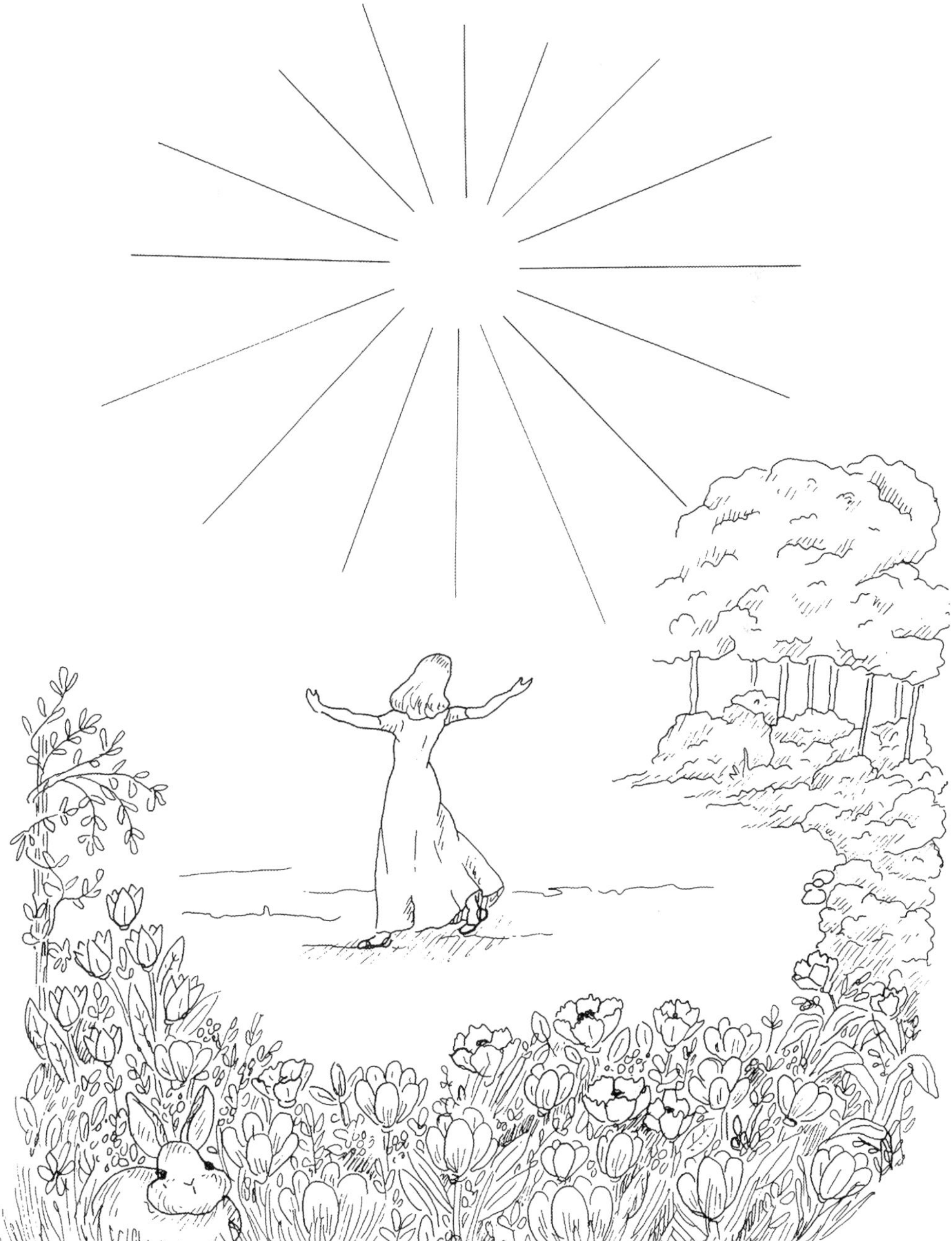

The Promise

Do not be dismayed, daughters, at the number of the things which you have to consider before setting out on this Divine journey, which is the royal road to Heaven. By taking this road we gain such precious treasures that it is no wonder if the cost seems to us a high one. The time will come when we shall realize that all we have paid has been nothing at all by comparison with the greatness of our prize.[34]

St. Teresa of Avila

It was one of those timeless, most sacred, moments. A group of people were gathered around a large rectangular table. There was a feeling of being engulfed in a bubble of Light and being transported into another world. It was very still and we all watched as the vision of a place called Heartlight Center began to unfold within our hearts. This was an open invitation, with nothing hidden. It was an opportunity to come together and behold a Life beyond our own self-created worlds. Our hearts felt true joy knowing the foundation of such a Life could only be total desire to know and live the Divine Will of God and to discover what it means to be One. Some felt they were like babes in a new world, yet feeling like it was so familiar. Others were instantly frightened and were certain there must be other secret motives for this whole vision of "life on the land" which was proposed, even if it had been talked about many times before. After all, doesn't everyone want something for themselves? So, a few vowed never to trust again. However, there were a few people who felt this was an ordained step which would allow something wondrous to occur. It was an invitation for a long-awaited door to be opened.

We could feel the entire planet holding its breath. Somewhere deep inside we knew that even if no one responded in the physical, it would not alter God's plan for what was about to happen. What a beautiful day it was! It was as if all the angels were singing a song of freedom.

We stood in awe as we witnessed God bring into manifestation the vision of this place called Heartlight Center, in His time and in His way. As each day passes, we understand more about His plan. Yes, it is true, as the sages have said; one must surrender all self-will before you enter into the world of Spirit, of Divine Love. We have all opened to understand the true nature of this mystery school called Heartlight Center. In the process, we have discovered that what is here has always been here. And what is more astounding, it has always been within our hearts. How free to know, for just a moment, that all we have been seeking for all our lifetimes has been within our very Beings forever. But in order to know that pure essence of our Divine nature, we must first surrender all that is not real – our past concepts, our judgments, our fears, our mistrust, and then embrace a world where God is the One in the Center, not our little selves. We are on the threshold of a great transformation in inner awakening. We cannot bring the old familiar world of form, of slavery with us. We must let it die.

The Promise

The mystery school at Heartlight Center is all-encompassing. Our meditations, mealtimes, service periods – all of our life is a classroom. We are dedicated to find what we are looking for – namely Truth. Each time a new experience is needed for deeper learning to take place, it always comes right at the exact time we need it. After living all these years together we can only stand at awe, seeing God's hand at work.

Yes - the invitation always goes out throughout this planet. Few respond. However, that will never alter the Reality of what Is. We are always free to choose to perceive what we wish. We are free to seek Truth or seek the shadows.

Through tears and rejoicing, through pain and ecstasy, there has been one changeless element continuously flowing through this land at Heartlight Center, as throughout creation. It is precisely that very Life, that Truth we seek to know. This year, it is time to be especially grateful for the opportunity given to us to live and experience the fullness of this Life here. Sometimes we tend to take it for granted. But, as long as we continue to want to be free, there will come a time when Spirit guides our steps that more of the mystery of Truth will be unveiled.

May all the opportunities and challenges be met with welcome hearts – knowing Love, Freedom, Truth, and, yes, Divine Union are all at the end. May this Center of Light we fondly call Heartlight Center continue to unfold within God's plan, according to His Divine Will. And, may it always be a Home for His Son.

So be it.

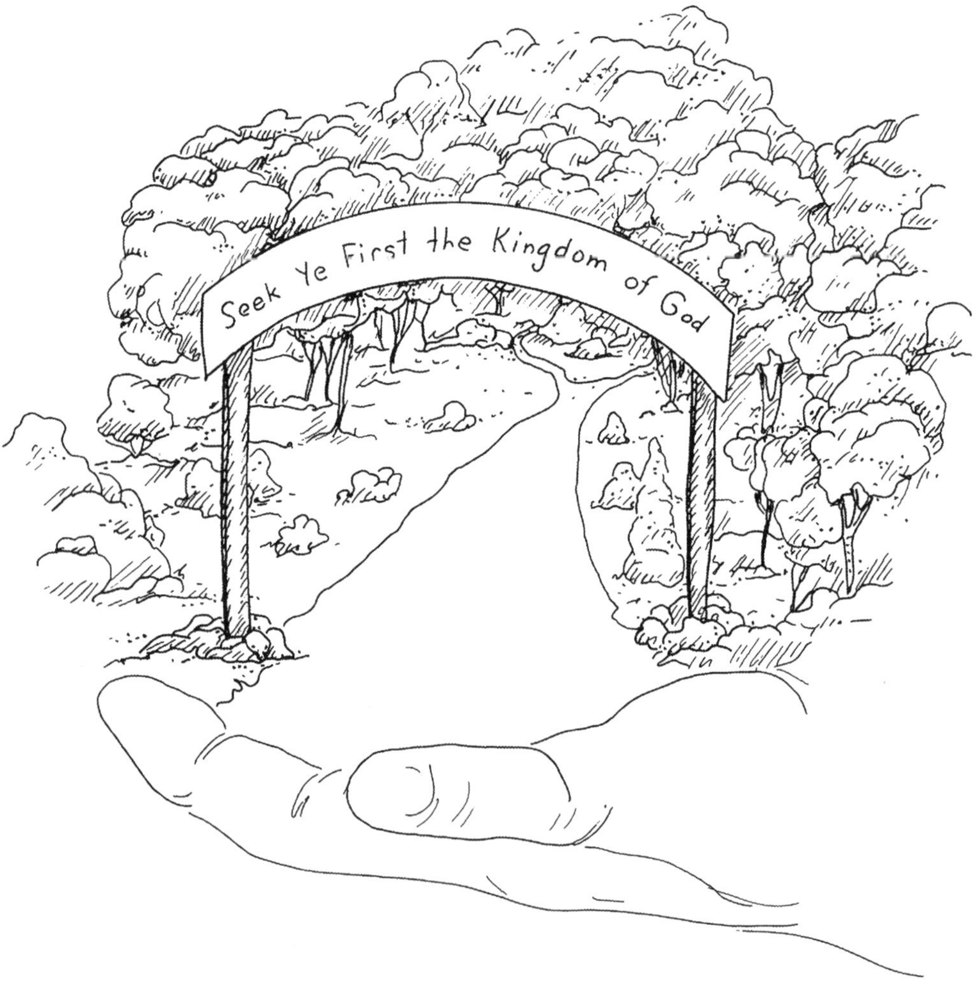
Seek Ye First the Kingdom of God

The Doe

Softly but quickly her attentive ears turned toward the sound of footsteps making their way up a newly made path through these woods she called home. Her four slender legs were planted firmly on the ground but she was ready to move in an instant to bound out of sight should they come too close. Her doe eyes strained and searched to see who was coming. She caught sight of them. They were a group who were smiling and laughing as they made their way deeper into the trees, single file. Occasionally they would help one another up the steep slopes or over the fallen tree trunks across the path. These creatures were different than those who had come before, she thought. There had been others who found their way into these woods, but when she heard this noise, a friend of hers would fall to the ground never to get up again. None of the creatures who were now coming up the path carried those noise makers, but they did have some other things.

She watched unnoticed, as they came to a clearing. A large hole had recently been dug there. They gathered in a circle around this opening in the earth and held one another's hands. What was this beautiful sound she heard? Where was that coming from? She listened again and moved a little closer but not so close as to be seen. Yes, it was coming from the group. What a lovely sound they were singing. She felt the sound going through the trees and into her own body and felt a part of the sound. It was in harmony with her own vibration. The sound ended and the group began to work around this opening in the earth, digging, raking, measuring, hammering, and happy in their work. Very cautiously and silently she moved away and back to her own group who were wondering where she had been so long.

Day after day they came and she watched from a distance as they worked. Each time they came, this gentle creature of the woods could feel their harmony with her kingdom and the plant kingdom. They would sometimes talk to the plants. Her tiny hooves would carefully carry her closer to them at each visit – but they still didn't see her.

The happy group continued with their endeavors and a structure grew. First, a foundation came. A hum of harmony radiated as walls were built. The gentle doe watched as the group came together time after time, and each time they began in a circle and sang that wonderful sound. Finally, three walls were raised from the ground, sloped into one another, and formed a point at the top. The doe watched the group work together lifting these strangely shaped sides. They seemed so few and the walls looked so heavy. But up they went with ease.

Laughter rang out and happiness filled the air whenever they came to this spot. How unlike those first people she had known. There was a difference about these creatures, she thought. There is a peaceful presence about them. She felt good to be here close by. Something radiated from them as they worked. It was different in the woods since they had come to this land. She was not afraid of them and actually felt a sense of peace she didn't understand. Other creatures on the land also were beginning to change and came closer to the work

The Doe

site and the group. Even the plants and trees felt a oneness with them. The fear the doe once knew had begun to leave. She felt free to venture closer.

The work continued into the fall season. Snow came and the structure was almost done. Now the group would come in the darkness. Single file they would silently make their way along the forest path, each with a light to show their way to the building which was now enclosed and warm inside. At night they didn't work but would enter this strange-looking shape, so the fragile doe could no longer see them. She would then hear their sound emanating wonderfully into the night and would listen, feeling it vibrate through the trees and upward into the sky. She enjoyed the sound through her being and felt at peace. Silently they came out and once more their single lights could be seen moving along the path and away, fading gradually into the night until she could no longer see them. Only a feeling of Love remained.

This land has changed, she thought. It once was a place where one had to be careful and watchful of those who would come to take and to hurt – of fearful noise. No more do we need to run and hide when man walks these paths. Peace has come to this place. I wonder, she thought, is it like this beyond this land? She gracefully leapt into the air and through the trees. She was going to that beautiful place in the woods where that strange 3-sided building stood and there she would feel love flow, not only through her but throughout all the forest and beyond.

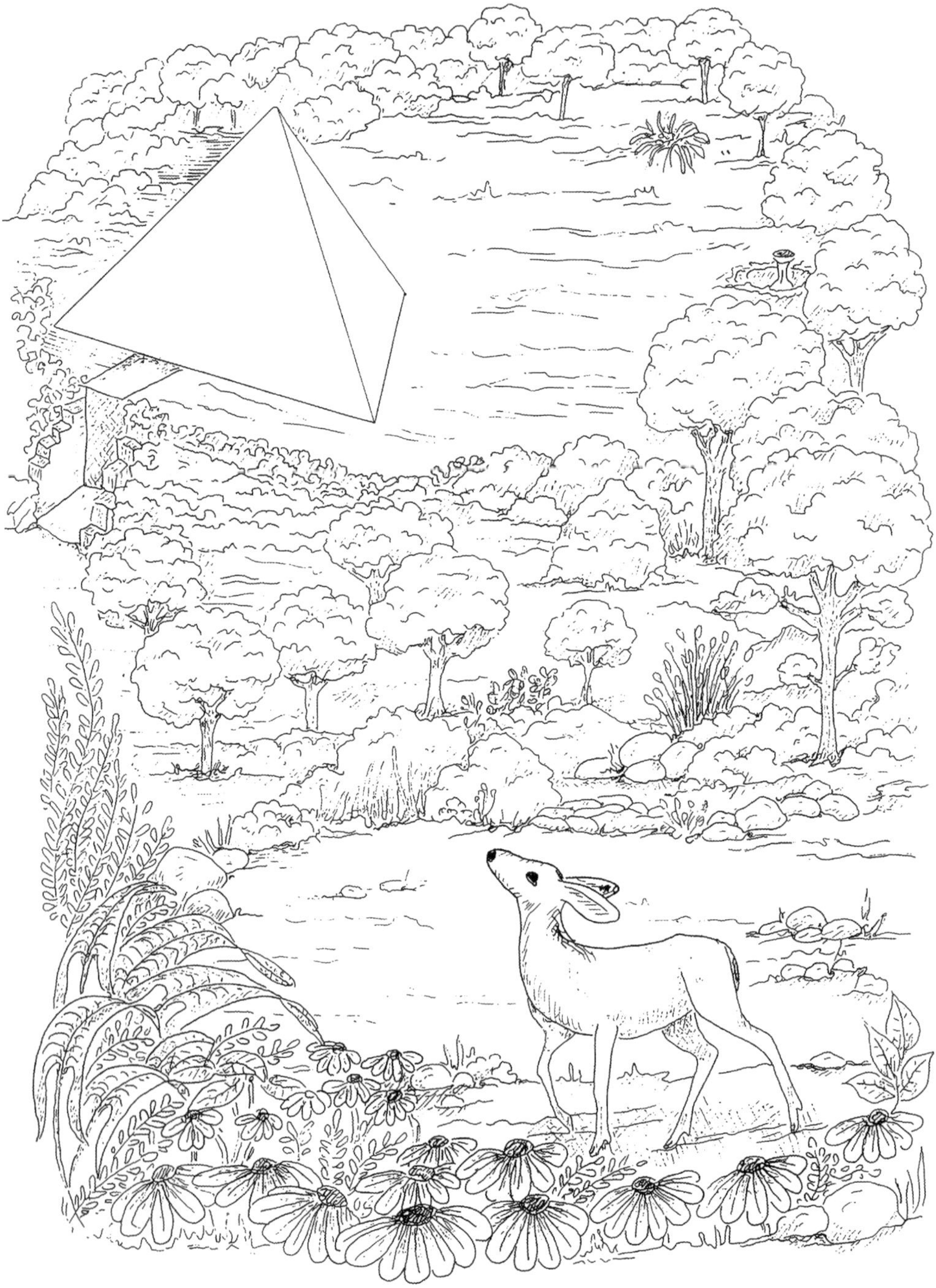

Time to Live

Springtime is such an exhilarating season of the year. It brings hope to all hearts as we see the trees bursting open, full with fragrant blossoms, and little bulbs whose stalks push courageously through newly-thawed soil. This time of the year holds such mystery, such magic. We are always reminded by this sudden beauty of nature that inside of us is that same pure expression of love and the same determination to manifest it. Every year, without exception, a wondrous event takes place. As if by some miracle, nature appears to wake up from a deep slumber, almost from a death-state. Slowly, and with intense focus, all of nature comes alive. Doesn't this tell us something and wouldn't this certainly inspire us? No matter what things look like or how lifeless we feel, beyond those strong thought-forms of sleep or death, there is always Life, God's very essence. We can always open to this reality, and as a result, our entire outer expression will inevitably change.

When we look at our own blossoming, our own awakening to life, it is just as magical as that of a tree. At one point, we reclaim with total honesty and with great fearlessness, "I want to live Life." From then on, we do not need to indulge in looking back and longing for moments past, but rather we seek to be dissolved in the eternal moment of the present.

It is so inspiring to walk by a huge oak tree during the most frigid period of the year, when all nature crackles with the coldness of the air, and to then touch this tree, hard and brittle, with snow all around the base. With our eyes, we see no apparent life. But contained within that entire structure, even at that very moment, in subfreezing temperatures, is a magnificent oak tree in total beauty, with the Life-force, the Love of God flowing through each one of its cells. The tree touches our hearts as it responds in its way to our loving gestures. We can feel life, the presence of the Father totally within it, even if it looks barren. It is, at the same time, in total perfection, bushy, alive and producing acorns for the next generation of oak trees. Can we not see that perfection in all creation as we do within the tree? How real the world is when we behold the presence of God in all. We can only be overcome with joy at the outward manifestation of Divine life. It is time we wake up to this reality of life within us, to accept our birthright, our True essence – pure, alive and total Joy. As we observe all the incredible signs of spring appearing, let spring also come within our very hearts. Let us take that next step into life and see ourselves, each other, and all creation as wondrous expressions of Love, all desiring in the depths of our hearts, to manifest only what is real. Yes, it is now time to finally Live. Let it be so.

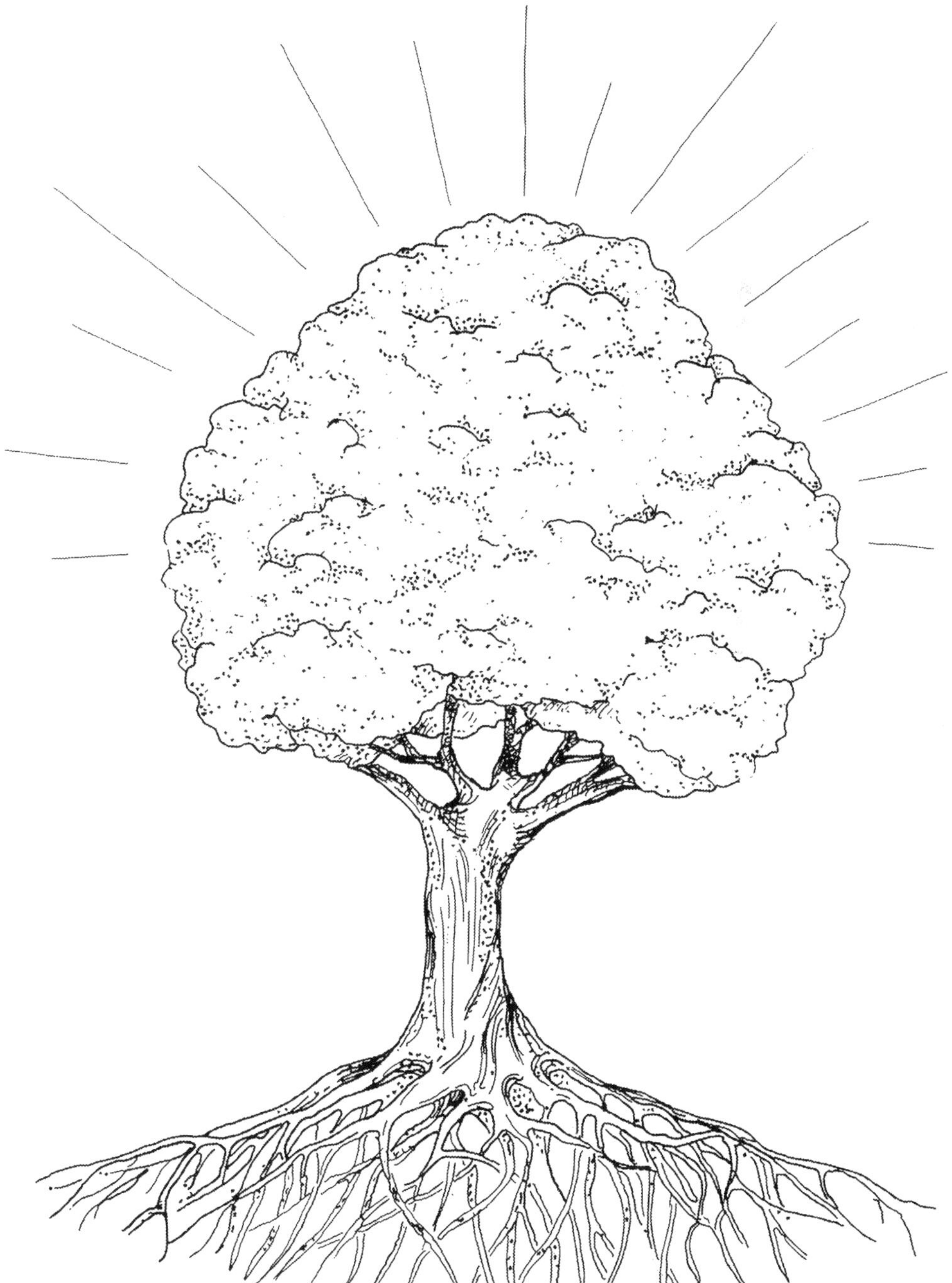

Epilogue

Who am I? Why am I here? What is my Life?

These are the questions that reverberate through humanity as we find ourselves on a planet filled with challenges. We are facing an evolutionary leap and as Spiritual Beings in physical bodies, we seek to know what our next steps are. We long to awaken from a deep slumber and claim our Heritage as Children of God. We would like to share a prayer which flows deep within our Souls and may touch yours, as well.

Heavenly Father, Divine Light of All, may this prayer reflect Your Infinite Will and touch the true desires of our hearts.

We have seen with our hearts the beauty of this planet, as it was in the beginning, ready for life, waiting for Your breath to bring forth such unique and beautiful Life forms, which would then glorify and make known Your Presence to all. A small butterfly dancing in the gentle breeze, emerald stalks of grass interweaving with one another, an innocent young maid with eyes turned upwards, a strong young man filled with pure life – these are but a few elements within Your Kingdom on this beautiful planet.

Unto the Least of These

One day a small boy looked up into the heavens, and his heart was filled with wonder. He could see faces in the clouds, and hear voices in the winds, and feel magic in the sunlight upon his face. Sitting down quietly in a grassy meadow, he saw life all about him. He watched with fascination as busy ants came to and fro, bearing loads far beyond their own weight, carrying food and provisions back for the colony. Each one seemed to know his own part, and there was an order and purpose in all their movements. He listened to the gentle song of the robins and the friendly chattering of the squirrels. He looked deep into the tall sweet grass and could see tiny insects of every imaginable form and variety. So much life, so seldom seen. He strolled over to the place where his dog lay sleeping in the shade of a maple tree, and thought how much he loved him. Then, curling up beside him on the warm earth, he too fell asleep, and in his sleep, he dreamed.

He saw a small group of people gathered by the side of the river, amidst the trees. They were seated on the ground and were engaged in a reverent conversation. He walked over, sat down on the outer edge of the circle, and listened …

"Tell us about him," said a young woman, with a look of desperate hope in her eyes.

"He spoke with an authority unlike any we had ever heard," answered the bearded man (who seemed to be some sort of teacher). "He brought Light to the Law of the Prophets, and fulfilled all their prophecies of the Anointed One ... the One for which all the world has waited."

"You knew him!" said one of the younger men in the circle, with an enthusiasm that was apparent to all.

"I was graced to have been with him for the past two years," the man with the beard answered humbly.

"Did he really do all those things that they say he did?" asked one of the elderly women. "Like healing the afflicted? ... " The boy noticed her hands were twisted and her limbs were weak and lifeless in appearance.

"Or like eating dinner with tax collectors and people of the streets? ... " chimed in another, before the teacher could reply.

"And casting out demons," said yet another. "And what about that man he raised from the dead? Was he really dead, or only sleeping? ... " asked one more.

"Peace ... peace ... " said the bearded traveler. "One at a time ..."

"Then you tell us," said one of the women, "tell us your most treasured memory of him."

After a long, thoughtful moment, the man gave an answer. His eyes were soft and gentle, like a newborn fawn. "It is not a tale you would know," he said quietly. "It was Passover in Jerusalem," he continued. "We had shared the meal together in the home of a trusted friend. One of the others and myself were discussing which of us should sit at his right hand on the

Throne of Glory when he overheard us and said: 'My brothers, let he who is the greatest among you be the servant of all[35] ...' And then, he knelt down before us and washed our feet, all of us ... Imagine, on his knees before us, washing our feet ... " The man's voice trailed off as a stillness fell upon them all. The boy, watching from the edge of the circle, saw tears in the teacher's eyes. And his heart was moved with wonder ...

"There was nothing in the world stronger than his gentleness," the teacher went on. "It was not easy for us to understand this, especially when it concerned our so-called enemies. For, as you know all too well, the soldiers committed every kind of atrocity against our friends and families. When we pressed him about this, he said: 'I send you out like sheep among wolves. Be, therefore, as wise as serpents, but, as harmless as doves.'[36]"

"But surely you were protected? ... "replied one of the listeners.

"As are all God's children," answered the man. "He loved us no more than he loves you – each is precious to him."

"Was he really as clever as they say in responding to the questions and charges of his opponents?" asked a young man eagerly.

"No ... " the teacher said slowly, his eyes looking deeply into those of the young man. "He was not clever, not in the way you mean. He spoke with wisdom, directed straight to the heart of their soul. He was not concerned with their debates and opinions of mind. He came for their souls, and it was to their souls he spoke."

There was silence for a time, each one reflecting within their own heart upon what the coming of this great soul had meant – not only to themselves but to the world. Then another spoke up. "How wonderful it must have been to know him – to be part of such a high and holy adventure, to have seen so many miracles and wonders! How I wish I could have met him!"

"I met him once," said a voice which had not spoken until now. The young boy who sat upon the edge of this circle listening, looked around to see who had just spoken. There, on the other side of the circle upon the riverbank, sat another young boy about his own age. He looked so very familiar somehow. He listened intently as this other boy spoke.

"I met him once, as he journeyed through our village."

"Be still, child," said one of the women. "Let the teacher speak." "Yes, we want to hear more from the teacher," agreed some of the men. The boy was silenced, and his eyes fell at once upon the ground.

Then the teacher said, in a tone more stern than they were expecting, "Let the boy speak. He too has a story to tell."

Though they were surprised at this response, the listeners gave way and fell quiet before the child. The little boy's eyes caught those of the bearded man, who nodded gently toward him. "Go on," he said kindly …

"My sister was very sick with a fever, and we were all afraid. Most of us were crying. I ran through the village to the place where he was speaking. I just knew he could help her. But so many were gathered around him, and they were all so tall. I could hardly see him, and no one would let me through. Finally, I got close enough to call out to him, but so many were asking questions of him and talking among themselves that no one paid any attention to me. Someone even said I should go back home, that this was of no concern to me. They said I was too little to understand.

I thought about it too, but I just couldn't leave. I knew he could help my sister. I just knew he could. Suddenly, he stopped speaking and turned his head and looked right at me. He beckoned me forward, and I came. I tried to speak and tell him why I had come. But my mouth was dry, and my heart was pounding. I couldn't say a word. I just looked into his eyes. They were so kind.

Then he took me in his arms and hugged me to his breast and sat me down in his lap, as he again spoke to the crowd. Do you know what he told them? ... He said, 'I tell you all solemnly, that unless you change and become like little children, you will never enter the Kingdom of Heaven.[37] And so, the one who makes himself little, as this little child, is the greatest in the Kingdom of Heaven.' Well, when he finished speaking, I felt so happy inside. I ran all the way back home to tell my family of what had happened. I was sure now that there was hope for my sister. When I got home, my sister met me at the door, with a big smile and tears in her eyes. The fever had left her, and she was well again. My sister, who had been ill so long, was well again ..." Here the boy stopped speaking and began to sob tears of gratitude.

"From this child and his simple faith," spoke the teacher to the circle, "you have learned of the heart of the Master's teachings: Love. You who wish you could have met him, you who wonder what it was like to be with him, you who long to know his touch – to you, I say in all truth, his Love is ever with you. And, it is only through Love that you can ever come to know him. Behold one another; see deeply into each other's heart, for it is there you shall find him. In the face of this young boy, in the tender touch of a mother's hand, in the comforting words of a friend; yea, even in the innermost heart of your so-called enemy – there you shall find him. We are the fruits of his great Love, and only by having the courage to live Love shall his orchard blossom forth into its full maturity. And remember what he told us, and what this young child has shown us so well: 'Whatsoever you do unto the least of these, you do also unto me.'[38]"

Once more a hush fell upon the circle, as the man with the beard looked upon them. Then, as the young boy who listened from the edge of the circle watched, everything began to fade from his sight, everything except the eyes of the teacher. They seemed to be looking right at him, and a voice within his own soul seemed to speak through the man's eyes: "My son, the time has come. Go back to your own world and remember. Remember to Love …"

"Remember," the boy said as he began to awaken upon the meadow. He opened his eyes and stretched slowly. There beside him sat his ever-faithful companion, tail wagging, eyes smiling. "Come on, boy," the youngster said as he arose, "We've got a lot to do today."

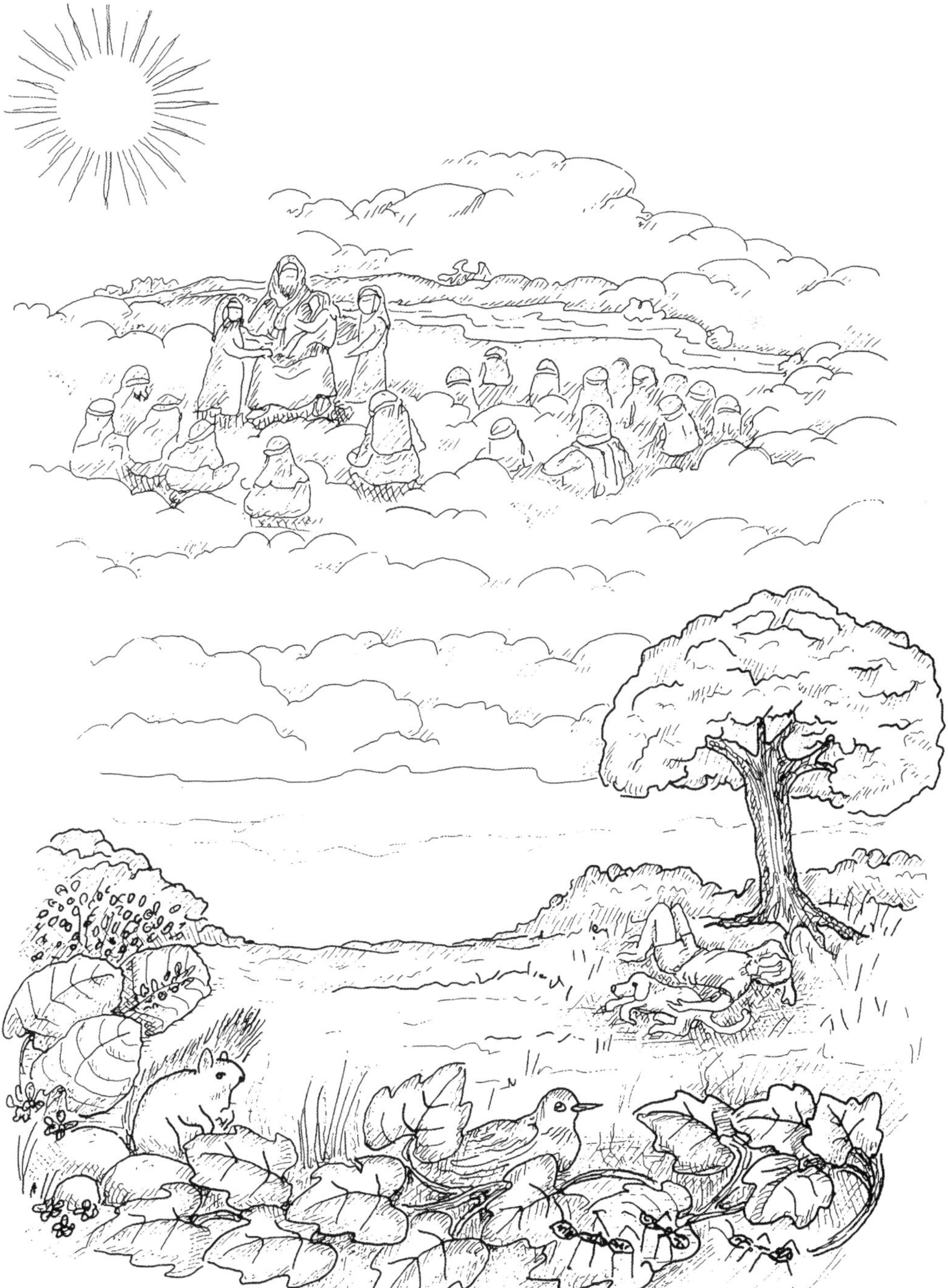

The Dream Restored

"Oh, dear God, how can it be written in words what it means to lose all awareness of our little self and wake up to being absorbed in You forevermore? How can Your Love within be transferred to another's heart so perfectly that no one wishes to claim it for themselves?" Those were Sharise's questions. She had gotten up very early that morning, even before the sun. Setting out on the narrow path up her favorite hill which led to the jagged mountains close by where she lived. She had had one of those dreams again and it had managed to keep her awake most of the night.

For many years she had the same dream come to her during times of great change within her life. It always began the same way. It was like this:

Sharise was a very peaceful, gentle soul, yet full of life which radiated throughout her. She was living a joy that most people only dreamt of. She was wed to a handsome man, quiet and very much awake in their One Life. They were never apart from one another. What was so special was that they were joined by their unquenchable passion for God. They were so in Love with God that it was said that some people saw them turn into millions of tiny sparkling suns as they talked with God in the quietude of their Hearts. They would literally vibrate, embraced in ecstatic Love for God, and would melt one into the other until only one shining Light could be seen – not two forms at all. When they reappeared and spoke with anyone nearby, it was said, that any disharmonious thought or distorted concept about Love, would have the chance to be transformed into thoughts of Reality. But one day, they met a young man, a visitor, who had traveled from a very long distance. In a moment, he would change their lives. He, too, spoke about God and about the love he felt for that divine presence within. But, every time he spoke, there was a chilling coldness that stabbed at Sharise's heart. She did not know why. She found herself troubled at times which, of course, was a brand new experience for her.

One day, as Sharise and her husband stood upon their favorite hill sharing in ecstasy their Love for God, the young man, the visitor, passed by them. He had heard of this occurrence from the many villagers, and he had witnessed changes in people as they had been in their presence while this was happening. There were a few villagers gathered about the couple on that very day. This visitor gazed upon the villagers and then witnessed the ecstatic Union of God which radiated Love through the hearts of all present. Something snapped within him and he began to grow very large, like a cold, dark cloud. He seemed to overpower the union of Sharise and her husband. However, this only occurred in the sight of the villagers. Suddenly, it was as if the Life-force drained out of all things. Sadness filled the air. The visitor smiled and repeated in a most cold voice, "Now you will learn of death." Then the stunned couple and the villagers watched him disappear as quickly as he had come. This was always when Sharise woke up, trembling and sobbing from this most disturbing dream.

Today, she was so distraught that she had run out of her house and with all her strength, had climbed to the very top of the hill, where she always felt safer. Now she was yelling with every fiber of her being to be released from this dream and be set free. She knew this husband of her dreams was real, but more real was their Love for God. She touched, for just a moment, what it felt like to let go of all knowledge of herself, to surrender her own will, and to be absorbed in the One Divine Will of God. "Thy will be done, God, in us and through us! I do not need to accept death anymore. I accept Life ... Your Eternal Life, forevermore."

Standing with arms outstretched and heart open – unprotected, simple, and radiating – something wonderful began to happen. It was as if a million suns enveloped Sharise and danced all around her form. She began to tingle, then grew weak and finally let go and exploded also into a million tiny suns, disappearing and pulsating within and all around. This formed a giant shimmering Light – gently singing from deep within itself:

> "Welcome Home, dear children. Welcome Home. Follow your heart and Embrace Love. There is no death – only Life. And that goes on and on – unto eternity. We are One. May God be glorified forevermore."

And so it was that beautiful day on this sacred hill, Sharise accepted what was real. She was released from her dream and woke up to find herself united with Love.

People still talk about that day they all saw this brilliant explosion of Light coming from the hill where Sharise stood, and how suddenly they all felt so much love in their hearts for everyone, and most especially for God. Yes, they had finally learned there was no death – only Life in God the Infinite One.

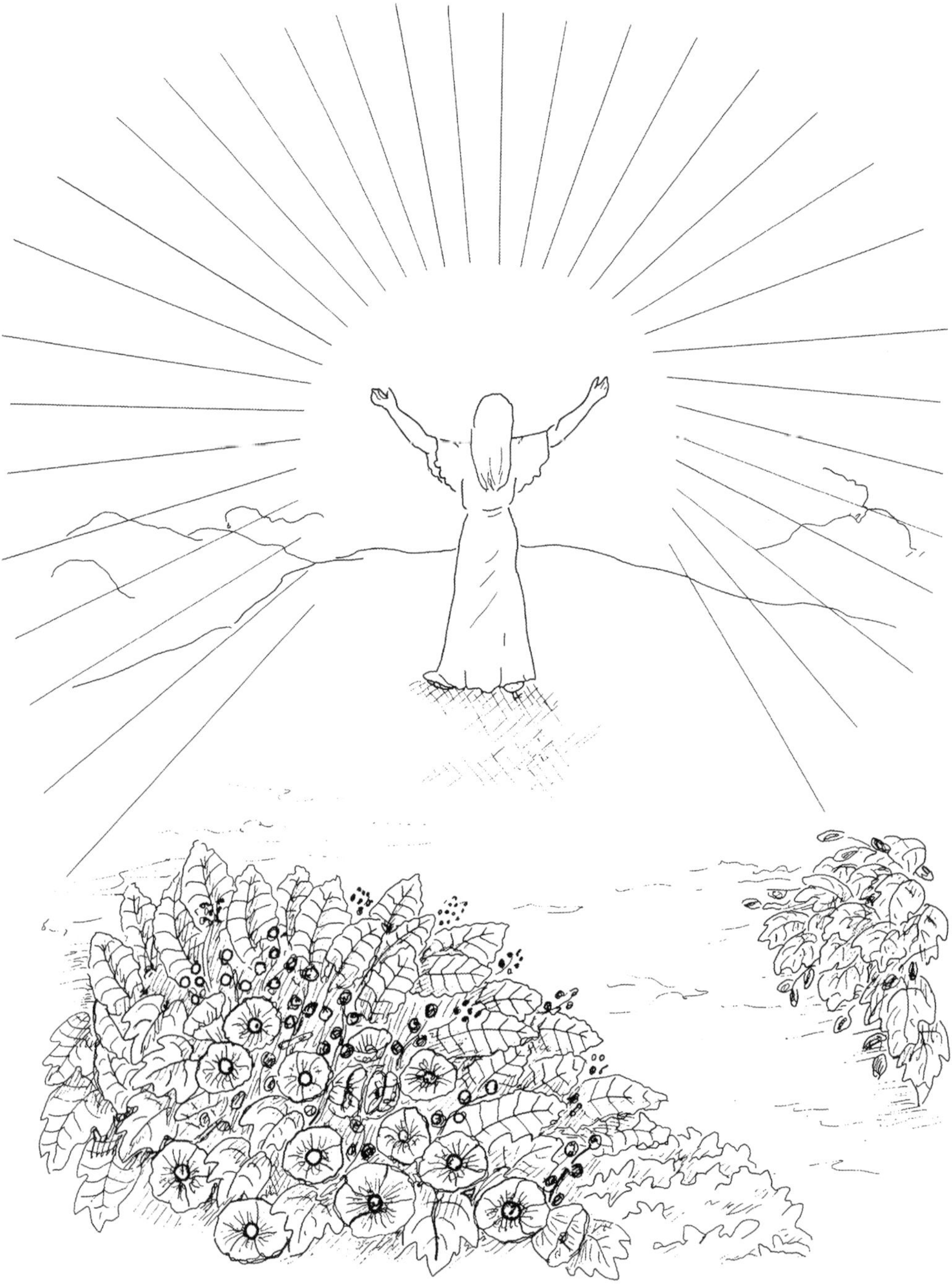

Please, Where is Love?

Once, in the time of shadows, lived a very gentle, yet curious young man, named Ohmram, with his beautiful, eternal companion, Eliaah. Often, they stood together at night listening to the call of Love which was carried by the wind into their hearts. One evening, just as the sun slipped beneath the horizon, they heard something different in the sound. It struck a note deep within. It was a cry they could not forget. Something had happened to that sound of harmony on the wings of the wind. It rang of sadness, yet was tinted with a vibration of longing, of searching. They looked at one another and knew it was time to go in search of the sound.

Without another thought, they left everything and departed from their peaceful abode. They traveled for many years following that cry, never being able to quite touch it in its fullness. "Why with all this beauty, with all this show of Love from God, The Infinite One, was there so much sadness, so much disharmony?" Those thoughts kept penetrating their heart until one day they found themselves standing in a silent meadow in a valley surrounded by majestic, snow-capped mountains. A cloud came down and enveloped them, carefully lifting them upwards. They felt the cloud bringing them to a spot which might help them to understand this penetrating cry, this sound which they had been constantly hearing. Suddenly, as if in a dream, they found themselves looking at the beautiful earth as if from a great distance away.

The earth began to spin, and then it was as if it stopped just long enough for Ohmram and Eliaah to zoom in on different areas of the planet and experience life at that moment. Each scene they witnessed, they also lived with all of the participants.

At first, they saw a young man strapped down with a rifle and other weapons, sitting under a tree, tired, hungry, and lost. He could not see any more reason to fight. He had made up his mind he could not kill again. He sat amongst corpses and blood and wondered who these nameless people were. Why must we hate one another? Why must we fight one another? For what? Who wins if someone loses his life? Who wins and why? No, he couldn't take another step in that direction. He had seen too much anger, too much hatred of his fellow man to ever feel that that was the way towards peace. There must be another way. He vowed even if he was tortured or beaten, he would never hurt another living creature. This was not the way. He would stand straight and not hate again. And then he cried and cried and cried – such a painful sound, such a deep sound. It was as if he was calling out for help. "Please let there be Love, let me know Love once more, let me feel a part of this world and embrace my brother soldiers and all others as my dear friends."

Ohmram and Eliaah recognized this sound, this cry. It was what called them forth from their home. And, there were other scenes which touched their hearts. They saw the panicked eyes of a newborn baby who was just abandoned, who cried out with confusion and pain, "Why was I left? Where is Love now? Help me to forgive, to live without feeling unwanted and forgotten. Help me to show love and not stop it. I came here to love, to trust, not to mistrust. Please, where is Love?" And the Light enveloped the earth, touching the young soldier, the newborn babe, all of nature, the small kitten, and then it permeated the heart of all humanity. For a moment, just for a moment, the earth looked like their home. It glowed with Love, Union, and Harmony. A smile came over their lips. They gazed deep into each other's eyes. Yes, they would stay until that sound which called them forth would be transformed freely and thus vibrate to the sound of Divine Love. Yes, they would stay.

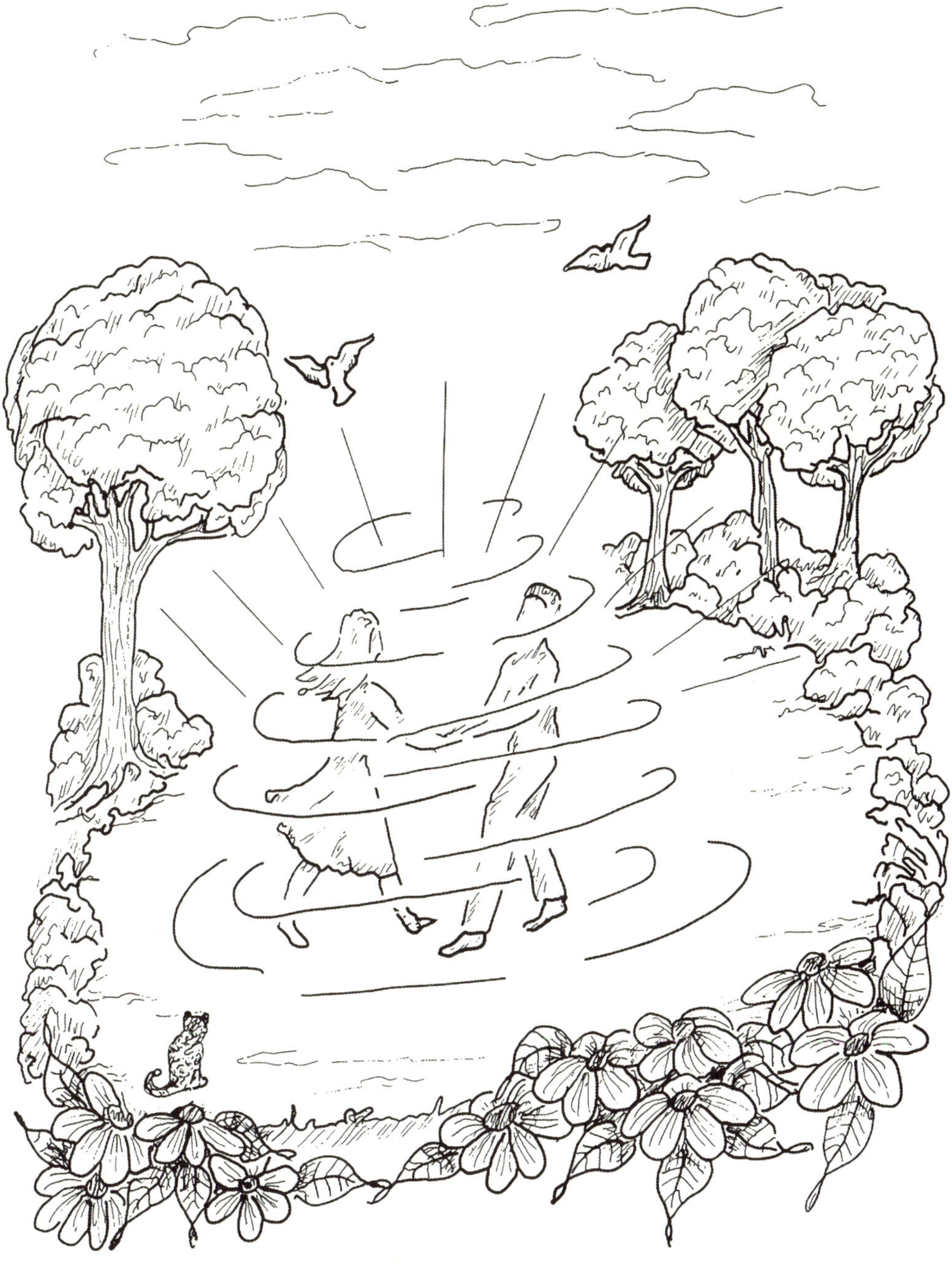

The Journey Home

There it was again. Yes, he heard it clearly now. He could even make out the words. "Come home … come home," said the voice. Sashal had been jolted awake several times during the night, for he thought he had heard whispering sounds. To his surprise, each time he woke up he had not found anyone in his room. But this time was different. Now he had even understood the words. He got up from his bed and began to get dressed. He felt really strange as if something important was about to happen.

"Come home … Come home!" It was as if those very words picked him up, carried him, and sat him in a chair in the middle of his room, his world. Sashal cried out in protest, "I don't understand! This is my home!" With that, he slumped over and cried uncontrollably, as if he was about to face something he had put off for a very long time. After several minutes, he regained his composure, bravely opened his eyes, and looked up. His whole room had changed. It was like he was sitting in the middle of a lush green meadow with hundreds of bright flowers swaying in the breeze. He saw a young boy, about seven years old, playing in the grass, hopping, and skipping to the rhythm of the wind. The little boy was swinging his arms up and down, trying to fly like his friends, the birds, and wondering why this feat was limited to birds and insects when it seemed it should be so natural for everyone to be able to fly. Suddenly, in the middle of one of his attempts at flight, he did a somersault just above the flowers and landed smoothly on his back. Then he looked up to study the cloud formations, something he really loved to do. He fixed his gaze on one giant cloud which seemed so shiny, almost alive. It moved gracefully, yet mysteriously across the skies. It got closer to him and seemed to stop right over him. He could feel his heart beating faster as he strained to pierce through the cloud to see a shape, a form, anything that might be inside of it.

The next thing he knew, he was aware of a gentle Being of Light coming forth through this cloud. It felt so familiar as if someone had opened a door to something which had been a part of him before time itself. There was no fear, just an underlying excitement to discover what this was all about. With no resistance, he began to float upwards within this beam, carried by the Light itself. Soon, he found himself in a chamber that radiated living colors and emanated soothing sounds, like a collective hum. He looked around and discovered he was placed right in the center of this wonderful chamber. He became very aware of the presence of a Being in the chamber, and upon turning to the right, he saw a most glorious Light which was shimmering. Progressively, he began to see the actual form of this Being of Light as it materialized. The emotions which went through the young boy at that moment were almost more than he could bear. Then, he thought he heard this Being of Light say something. The words permeated the young boy's whole body as if each cell responded in some way to certain sounds that seemed to be directed toward his heart.

"My Son," began the Being of Light, "I have waited for this moment for quite some time. Some day you will not think of this meeting as a faint dream in the past, you will know of its Reality. I was there when you first chose to come to this Emerald planet, to experience life through this form of matter, to serve and to Love in innocence and goodness. I was with you as you set about to live the Truth, to express total Love. I was even with you at the times of deepest despair when you shouted in utter desperation for you felt so vulnerable, so alone because you could not recognize anything. Nothing seemed the same. It was as if a dark fog had overtaken all that was familiar, and you were lost. For one moment there was no hope. I was there, pleading for you to look within to that gentle, untouched spot within, which held the key for your Freedom from that all-encompassing abyss of pain. You began your journey Home then. Now you are ready for the next step on this glorious adventure, where all the memories, the thoughts which have served to keep you slave to this illusionary world of separation will be exhausted in the Light of Reality. You, dear One, are ready. You have called from your Heart, and it is time to Come Home … come home."

The chamber where the young boy sat seemed to expand and change, even in its appearance. Many other Beings of Light appeared, and he witnessed a Life that was expressed through them that was so infinitely old and yet very familiar to him. In the span of seconds, he had not only observed Life, but it seemed he had lived it as well. He just knew it was Real. Those Beings desired nothing for themselves. They seemed to be so filled with a Love which was expressed through them, and at the same time, their only thought was to glorify the Source of that Love. How could words express what he was feeling at that time?

Once more, the Being of Light spoke. He said, "You will remember when it is time. Then you will have all the courage to take that final step across the unknown. You will feel the emptiness of illusion filling you with despair and will finally turn within, to find the Sacred Temple of the Heart, where you and God have always dwelled as One. This is your journey, dear One." And once again, with a most penetrating yet gentle voice, the Being of Light repeated, "Come Home! Come home!" Instantly, the young boy found himself back in the meadow. He looked up quickly and saw that the cloud was slowly gliding away into the distance.

At that very same time, in a small room, Sashal let out a cry that extended beyond the Earth. Through the sounds of his sobs, he uttered, "Now I remember. I was that boy, many years ago. It was not a dream, I understand. I am ready now. I do wish to come Home!" With the lightness of someone who had just been released from a cage of darkness, he got up, turned around, opened the door, and walked out of his room, leaving everything behind! For the first time in what seemed like eons, Sashal knew he was not alone. He was truly home.

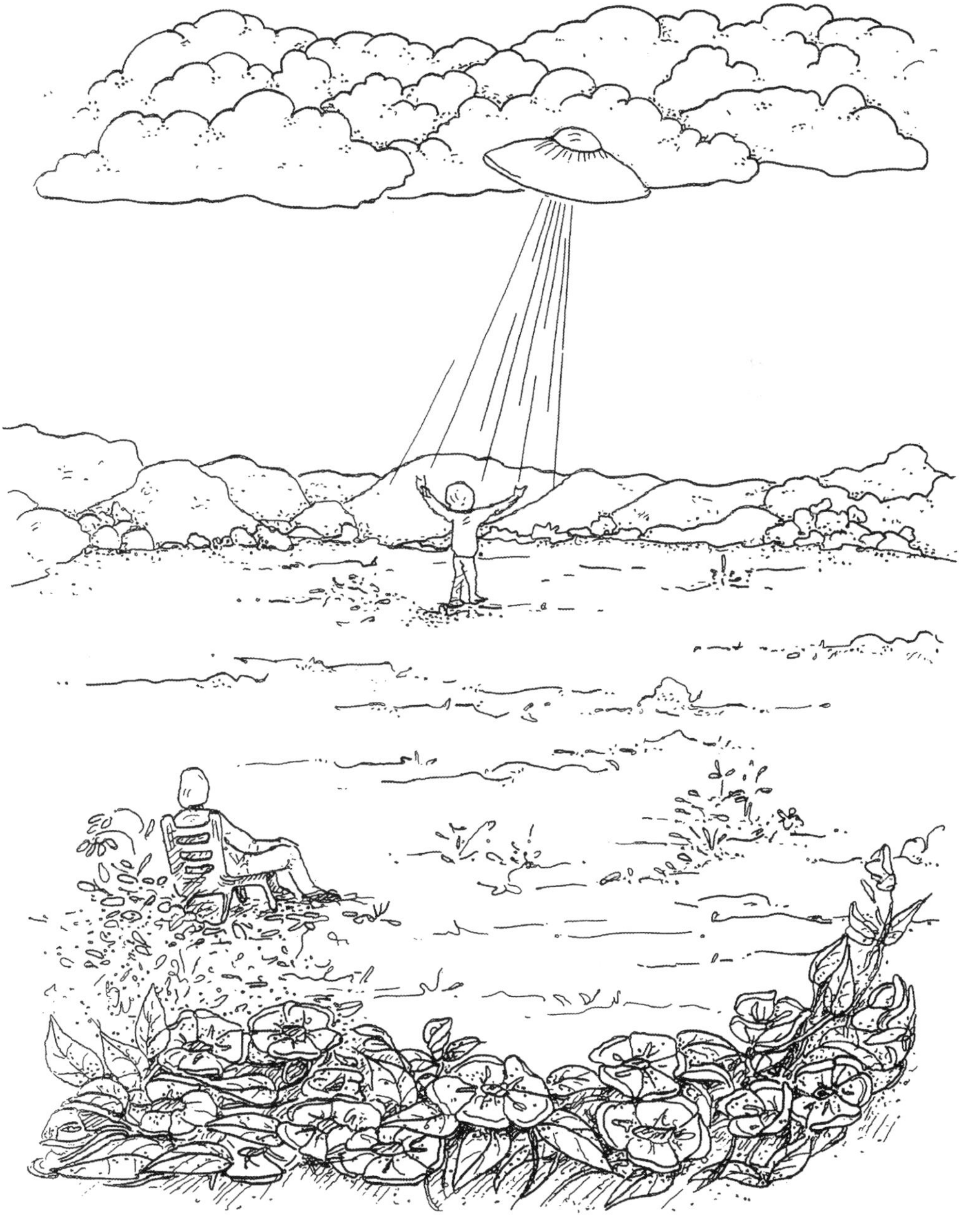

Please, Where is Love?

a deep penetrating sound of pain came from deep within her soul. She cried until the Earth shook in despair. Ohmram and Eliaah cried with her – a cry of Love, a cry which seemed to stabilize the trembling ground.

Then their attention turned to a scene of nature: animals, vegetables and minerals. Things were dying. They were changing color. Life was being drained out of the forms. Again, the cry was heard, "Where is Love? Show me Love. We have served man, and now we are used up. We are dying. We were meant to work together in harmony. Please, help. Where is Love? We are fading fast." They saw the eyes of a small kitten which were closed. This gentle creature had a most loving and forgiving smile – one of supreme patience. "Would those eyes ever open again?", thought Ohmram and Eliaah. "If they did, would they find a change? Would they find the Love they were yearning for?"

So many more scenes were experienced. Ohmram and Eliaah found themselves filled with the sound which came from the very heart of creation on this planet earth. "Where is Love? Please help me to find it. I want to know what it is. I cannot look away from Love anymore. I cannot look away from Peace, from Union, from God."

Ohmram and Eliaah had found the sound they were looking for. Memories of their quiet abode filled their hearts. Pictures of people helping each other, loving each other, and serving God passed through their minds. A dance, which they often did together, stirred in their hearts. They joined hands, hearts, minds, and spirit and began spinning around, chanting a song of Love. They were filled with Love for God. Round and round they danced, singing and lifting their vision ever higher until they saw One magnificent Light which radiated and extended out beyond infinity. With awe and humility, they watched as

When we search our hearts we see all life on this planet living in Peace, living harmoniously with one another, for we know we are not here to compete with or harm another, for we would then be forgetting that You are the very Spirit of All. To wish harm to another would only be a refusal to see Your Light in another part of Your creation.

Peace is within the grasp of this planet. We know it. We must accept to be an instrument of that Peace. When we see our brothers and sisters in pain, may we also see Your Light within them. When we feel the anger of confusion, may our hearts know Your Presence. When we lack the desire to heal the deep wounds of separation, may we feel Your patient understanding and Infinite Love. When we do feel alone, please help us to see the Son, all radiant and giving unconditionally, a life-line of Love. And, when we meet our brothers or sisters who have nowhere to put their heads at night, no spot to call their own, no food in their stomachs or clothes to keep them warm, please open the doors of compassion, so we might care for them and love them as You love us, and as Your Son has expressed that Love for all to see. May we realize how important it is that all people who dwell on this planet know that they are loved and that someone cares for them. May they never have to go to sleep feeling rejected or alone. May we always remember that each person here is your child, a Child of God, and each is to live in the dignity that is worthy of a Child of Light.

May we be open to accept the Light that we are, as a gift from You, a gift which is our very Life itself. Then, as we know it in ourselves, may we never be blind to its Presence within all our brothers and sisters and all creation. We cannot help but to then know of the reality of Your Kingdom on this planet, bathed in Your Light, unified by Your One Presence, and permeated with Love Divine.

May Your Divine Presence continue to be accepted and known upon this planet, for that alone will bring the Unity, Peace and Love so long awaited for. So Be It. It is So.

Many times this prayer has presented itself when we have cried out with an ache so deep that only the balm of the Voice of Love could satisfy. At those moments, we could only see a planet bathed in Love. And then questions came.

What if the world could hear the Voice of the Divine One, and what if we could hear it so clearly that it became the only language we spoke to one another? What if the sound of that Voice could reach around the world, dissolving all barriers, melting all distances, and flowing freely to every heart that would receive it? What if it could begin as the tiniest of seeds carried in from afar and take root on this planet, where it multiplied and flourished and prospered, until there was no land upon the earth where its sweet fruits did not blossom? What if it moves through all our circles of friends, acquaintances and neighbors and lands and nations – like a ripple on a giant pond, all begun from one still point within the very Center of All? What if this Voice could speak to the world and the world would understand? We know it can. May we all have the courage to respond to this Divine Voice of Love.

References

1 *Epigraph, p vii:* "*God expects but one thing of you, and that is that you should come out of yourself in so far as you are a created being and let God be God in you.*" - by Meister Eckhart, found in *Words to Live By,* Ecknath Easwaran, Nilgiri Press,1990, 1996, 1999, 2005, p 77

2 *A Child of God,* p 2: "*Lest ye become as little children, ye cannot enter the kingdom of heaven.*" - paraphrase of *Jerusalem Bible:* Matthew 18:3

3 Meister Eckhart quote, p 28: found in *Words to Live By,* Ecknath Easwaran, p 14.

4 *For One Soul, p 51:* "*Father, forgive them, for they know not what they do.*" - *KJV Bible,* Luke 23:34

5 *Prayer of St. Francis,* p 57: found in *God Makes the Rivers to Flow,* Ecknath Easwaran, Nilgiri Press, 1982, p 21

6 *In the Beginning, p 67:* "*I was created in love; therefore nothing can console or liberate me save love alone. The soul is formed of love and must strive to return to love. Therefore it can never find rest nor happiness in other things. It must lose itself in love. By its very nature it must seek God who is love*" - by Mechthild of Magdeburg, found in *Words to Live By,* Ecknath Easwaran, p 15. Merchild's words also found in her book, *The Flowing Light of The Godhead: The Revelations of Mechthild of Magdeburg,* by Mechthild of Magdeburg 2012 Reprint of Original 1953 Edition,

7 *I Am With You Always, p 77*: From *Ascent of Mount Carmel* by St. John of the Cross, Book 1, Chapter 11:4, as quoted in *Words to Live By*, Ecknath Easwaran, 1999, p 249.

8 *The Silent Visitor, p 82:* "Peace," the man spoke, "I give unto you, My Peace I leave with you." - paraphrase of *KJV Bible*, John 14:27

9 *The Year of Awakening, p 104*: *"the ego cage of I and mine,"* The Bhagavad Gita, Translated for the Modern Reader by Ecknath Easwaran, Nilgiri Press, 1985, p 69, and quoted in *God Makes the River to Flow* by Ecknath Easwaran, Nilgiri Press,1982,1991, p 37

10 *The Year of Awakening*, p 104: *"pass from death to immortality",* The Bhagavad Gita, Translated for the Modern Reader by Ecknath Easwaran. P 69, and quoted in *God Makes the River to Flow* by Ecknath Easwaran, p 37

11 *The Little Chalice, p 113*: *"But whosoever drinketh of the water that I shall give him shall never thirst; but the water that I shall give him shall be in him a well of water springing up into everlasting life."* - *KJV Bible*, John 4:14

12 *Love is Forever, p 116*: "Behold, I have come that the world would Know just how much I Love My Father. Now, I must follow My heart and do His Will. Come let us go." - paraphrase of *Jerusalem Bible*, John 14:31

13 *The Manger of the Heart, p 120*: *"Blessed are the pure of heart, for they shall see God."* - KJV Bible, Matthew 5:8

14 *Time for Change, p 124*: "Meister Eckhart says to let God be God in us." – paraphrase of quote from Meister Eckhart – found in *Words to Live By*, Ecknath Easwaran, p 77. Also found in *Meister Eckhart, The Essential Sermons, Commentaries, Treatises and Defense, Translation and Introduction* by Edmund Colledge, O.S.A. and Bernard McGinn, Paulist Press, 1981, p 184

15 *Ablaze with Love, p 127*: *"I know the path. It is straight and narrow. It is like the edge of a sword. I rejoice to walk on it. I weep when I slip. God's word is: 'He who strives never perishes. Though, therefore, from my weakness I fail a thousand times, I shall not lose faith."* - quote from Mahatma Gandhi, found in *Words to Live By*, Ecknath Easwaran,

p 115; original quote from *My Religion*, (Ahmedabad, India: Navajivan, 1955,) Mahatma Gandhi. P 30

16 Poem by St. Teresa of Avila, p 131: found in *God Makes the Rivers to Flow*, Ecknath Easwaran, Nilgiri Press, 1982, 1991, p 39

17 *This is the Day, p 138:* "I have come to show the world how much I love my Father." – paraphrase of *KJV Bible*, John 14:31

18 *This is the Day, p 139:* "I have come to show the world how much I love my Father." – paraphrase of *KJV Bible*: John 14:31

19 *I Am With You, p 142*: "My feet walk this planet now to show you how much I love my Father." – paraphrase of *KJV Bible*: John 14:31

20 *The Light of Love, p 145*: *"For unto us, a child is born."* - *KJV Bible*, Isaiah 9:6

21 *The Light of Love, p 147*: "My Father and I are One." – paraphrase of *Jerusalem Bible*, John 10:30

22 *Love Ye One Another, p 155*: *"In the beginning was the word."* - *Jerusalem Bible*, John1:1

23 *Love Ye One Another, p 156*: "Love God with all your heart, with all your soul, with all your mind, and with all your life." – paraphrase of *Jerusalem Bible*, Luke 10:27

24 *The Light of Love*, p 157: "Love ye one another, as I have loved you." - paraphrase of *Jerusalem Bible* quote, John 15:12

25 *Lead Me to the Real, p 167*: *"Lead me from the unreal to the real. Lead me from darkness to light. Lead me from death to immortality."* – *God Makes the Rivers to Flow*, Ecknath Easwaran, Nilgiri Press, 1982, 1991, p 30: Original found in The Brihadaranyaka Upanishad, in *The Upanishads*, Translated for the Modern Reader by Ecknath Easwaran, Nilgiri Press, 1987, p 33

26 *Paradise Found. P 173*: *"Be still and know that I Am God."* - *KJV Bible*, Psalm 46:10

27 *Paradise Found, p 173*: "seek the Kingdom of God first" - paraphrase of *KJV Bible*, Matthew 6:33

28 *Truth is the Way, p 175*: "*Truth is victorious, never untruth. Truth is the way; truth is the goal of life, Reached by sages who are free from self-will.*" - from The *Mundaka Upanishad*, in *The Upanishads*, Translated for the Modern Reader by Ecknath Easwaran, Nilgiri Press, 1987, p 116

29 *Once There Was a Man, p 181*: "*Father, forgive them; for they know not what they do.*" - *KJV Bible*, Luke 23:34

30 *Once There Was a Man, p 182*: quote by Meister Eckhart, found in *Original Goodness*, Ecknath Easwaran, Nilgiri Press, 1989, p 15

31 *Year of Acceptance, 186*: "*How gently and how lovingly Thou wakest in my bosom.*" - *Living Flame of Love*, St. John of the Cross, Translated & Edited by E. Allison Peers, Triumph Books, 1991, p 207-208

32 *Peace on Earth*, p 192: "*I call you friends because I have made known to you everything I have learnt from my Father. You did not choose me. No, I chose you, and I commissioned you to go out and to bear fruit, fruit that will last ... What I command you is to love one another.*" - *Jerusalem Bible*, John 15:15-17

33 *Loving God is All There Is, p 195*: "*I never ask God to give himself to me. I beg him to purify, to empty me. If I am empty, God of his very nature is obliged to give Himself to me to fill me.*" - *The Best of Meister Eckhart*, Edited by Halcyon Backhouse, The Crossroad Publishing Company, 1993, p 132

34 *The Promise, p 199*: "*Do not be dismayed, daughters, at the number of the things which you have to consider before setting out on this Divine journey, which is the royal road to Heaven. By taking this road we gain such precious treasures that it is no wonder if the cost seems to us a high one. The time will come when we shall realize that all we have paid has been nothing at all by comparison with the greatness of our prize.*" - *The Way of Perfection*, Teresa of Avila, Translated and Edited by E. Allison Peers, Image Books, Doubleday, 1964, p 150

35 *Unto the Least of These, p 213*: "My brothers, let he who is the greatest among you be the servant of all" - paraphrase of KJV Bible, Matthew 23:11

36 *Unto the Least of These, p 213*: "I send you out like sheep among wolves. Be, therefore, as wise as serpents, but, as harmless as doves.' – paraphrase of *KJV Bible*, Matthew 10:16

37 *Unto the Least of These, p 215*: 'I tell you all solemnly, that unless you change and become like little children, you will never enter the Kingdom of Heaven. And so, the one who makes himself little, as this little child, is the greatest in the Kingdom of Heaven.' – paraphrase of *Jerusalem Bible*, Matthew 18:3,4

38 *Unto the Least of These, p 216*: 'Whatsoever you do unto the least of these, you do also unto me.' – paraphrase of *Jerusalem Bible*, Matthew 25:40

Acknowledgements

We want to acknowledge the many tireless hours spent by so many people who proofed, edited and generally helped with the publication of this book. Without their happy participation and willingness to open to the vision of this book, it would not have been completed in such a beautiful fashion. We specifically wish to recognize and thank Millie DusSault, Christine Celani and Virginia Alexander who spent many hours proofreading, while smiling and crying as they read each story – many times. Thank you to Jeanette Haynes who embraced the task of drawing all these magnificent inspirational pictures you see throughout the book. Many hours were spent living the stories and letting them speak to her Heart as she drew what came to her. Roberta Jackson and David Alexander set out to work together on typing, editing, formatting and generally getting the finished manuscript ready for publishing. Their computer skills and absolute willingness to learn what was needed to publish a book was such a wonder to behold. Thanks to both of them for all that was done. What a Job! We want to thank both Virginia and David Alexander for the many hours spent on all the little things they did that pulled together the final draft of the book. We watched as many of these stories penetrated deep within their souls as they worked to get the book ready to touch and, perhaps, to inspire others to begin their own journeys.

We are most grateful to all of these beautiful people for their open Hearts and their willingness to Soar into the unknown.

We all lived this together.
What a wonderful gift!

About the Authors

Georges and Judith Arseneau are lifelong experiencers who teach classes in metaphysics and spiritual transformation. They are also coordinators for a Florida non-profit called Angels of Hope Love is Real, which is known for the projects Kids to Seniors, bringing seniors and kids together, and Kids to Kids, connecting children all over the planet. They currently live in Florida.

Printed in the United States
By Bookmasters